TOTAL

exposure

TOTAL
exposure

The Movie Buff's Guide to Celebrity Nude Scenes

JAMI BERNARD

A Citadel Press Book
Published by Carol Publishing Group

A Citadel Press Book
Published by Carol Publishing Group
Citadel Press is a registered trademark of Carol Communications,
   Inc.
Editorial Offices: 600 Madison Avenue, New York, N.Y. 10022
Sales and Distribution Offices: 120 Enterprise Avenue, Secaucus,
   N.J. 07094
In Canada: Canadian Manda Group, One Atlantic Avenue, Suite 105,
   Toronto, Ontario M6K 3E7
Queries regarding rights and permissions should be addressed to
Carol Publishing Group, 600 Madison Avenue, New York, N.Y. 10022

Carol Publishing Group books are available at special discounts for
bulk purchases, sales promotion, fund-raising, or educational
purposes. Special editions can be created to specifications. For
details, contact: Special Sales Department, Carol Publishing
Group, 120 Enterprise Avenue, Secaucus, N.J. 07094

Manufactured in the United States of America
10 9 8 7 6 5 4 3 2 1

Library of Congress Cataloging-in-Publication Data
Bernard, Jami.
     Total Exposure : the movie buff's guide to celebrity nude scenes /
   by Jami Bernard.
         p.   cm.
     "A Citadel Press book."
     ISBN 0-8065-1619-4 (pbk.)
     1. Nudity in motion pictures.   2. Motion picture actors and
actresses—Credits.   I. Title.
PN1995.9.N92B47   1995
791.43´653—dc 20   94-46536
                                                           CIP

To my sister Diane Bernard, an avid moviegoer and dear friend, who for reasons mysterious even to her paid good money to see *Conan the Barbarian* twelve times

Contents

INTRODUCTION
The Abiding Fascination With Romance, Sex, and Nudity on Film...ix

BARE ESSENTIALS
Nude Scenes That Helped Define a Career...1
Kim Basinger, Jennifer Beals, Annette Bening, Jacqueline Bisset, Phoebe Cates,
Laura Dern, Susan Sarandon, Christian Slater, Uma Thurman,
Kathleen Turner, Sigourney Weaver

SHOCK VALUE
Don't Tell Mom...43
Julie Andrews, Drew Barrymore, Linda Blair, Jamie Lee Curtis, Jeff Goldblum,
Charlotte Rampling, Isabella Rossellini, Mickey Rourke, Brooke Shields

FULL-FRONTAL ASSAULT
The Final Frontier...73
Ellen Barkin, Willem Dafoe, Jaye Davidson, Robert De Niro, Richard Gere,
William Hurt, Jeremy Irons, Don Johnson, Harvey Keitel, Nicole Kidman,
Julianne Moore, Theresa Russell, Eric Stoltz, Bruce Willis

NAKED AMBITION
Stars Who Disrobe at the Drop of a Hat, or Whatever...123
William Baldwin, Bo Derek, Jennifer Jason Leigh, Madonna,
Demi Moore, Sylvester Stallone, Sharon Stone

REGRETS ONLY

Stars Who Should Have Kept Their Clothes On...149

Dana Delany, Diane Keaton, k. d. lang, Sean Young

STRIPTEASE

Stars Who Won't Go All the Way, at Least Not Often Enough...165

Ann-Margret, Alec Baldwin, Tom Cruise, Jodie Foster, Liam Neeson,
Nick Nolte, Michelle Pfeiffer, Keanu Reeves, Julia Roberts,
Madeleine Stowe, Meryl Streep, Patrick Swayze

ART HOUSE NUDITY

Foreign Film Buffs...201

Victoria Abril, Isabelle Adjani, Antonio Banderas, Juliette Binoche,
Gerard Depardieu, Lena Olin

METHOD NUDITY

Stars Who Really Get Into the Act...225

Michael Douglas, Melanie Griffith, Linda Hamilton, Mariel Hemingway,
Elle Macpherson, Penelope Ann Miller

REAR PROJECTION

The Butt Stops Here...245

Kevin Costner, Mel Gibson, Woody Harrelson, Goldie Hawn,
Kurt Russell, Arnold Schwarzenegger

MEMORABLE SEX SCENES

Snapshot Album of Famous Sex Scenes in Movie History...265

WISH LIST

Stars Who Should and Should Not Undress...271

INDEX

...281

Introduction

The Abiding Fascination With Romance, Sex, and Nudity on Film

Like most people, I enjoy seeing actors get naked. But that's not why I wrote this book.

Well, let's say that's not *entirely* why I wrote this book. After all, contemplating sex scenes and poring over photos of cute stars and their moons is not the worst activity in the world.

But on a somewhat more serious side, as a film critic, I couldn't help noticing how many big-name celebrities were suddenly dropping their drawers. Hardly a movie would go by without seeing Michael Douglas's tush, Kim Basinger's breasts, Harvey Keitel's schlong. In 1994, two actresses with the highest pedigrees took the neckline plunge—Meryl Streep peeled off her Lycra for a nude swim, and Jodie Foster lounged like the White Rock girl. Sharon Stone's beaver shot in *Basic Instinct* is the single most valuable item on her resumé. Demi Moore can't be bothered with such mundane chores as wearing clothing for her magazine shoots, and her husband, Bruce Willis, has offered his sizable penis for big-screen inspection with the ease with which he might donate some *Die Hard* memento to Planet Hollywood. People who are justifiably proud of their bodies are quick to expose them, like Sylvester Stallone, but people we think should stay buttoned up for the common good are just as eager to drop trou, like Mickey Rourke. It's a veritable epidemic of epidermis.

Since nudity has always been an integral part of the movies—silent movies featured a stunning array of flesh—this cannot be passed off as some sort of fad like the Hula-Hoop. Stars are actively embracing nude scenes as symbols of their star status; it's like having their own Lear jet or getting first look at a script. They live in a community that puts a crushing emphasis on youth, beauty, and body tone, and if they have it, by golly, they're determined to flaunt it.

The typical career arc in terms of nudity now seems to be that in the beginning, actors do nude scenes because they can't afford not to—they don't have the clout to say no, and they need instant recognition (picture Phoebe Cates, as I'm sure you can, in *Paradise*). Then, when they're more established, they

Teenage Hedy Lamarr notoriously keeps everything afloat in the 1933 shocker *Ecstasy,* called "the stark naked truth of a woman's desire for love." Here is some of that stark naked truth.

Photo courtesy of Photofest

have the luxury of picking and choosing scripts, and they can avoid nude scenes completely (like Jodie Foster in mid-career) or call in a body double (as Demi Moore did in *Indecent Proposal*). Later, when they are superstars who no longer need the work, the prestige, or the money, again they turn to nude scenes to prove they are *such* serious actors that they can afford to do it for the sake of art (like Harvey Keitel or Robert De Niro).

Thanks to this career arc that brings nudity full circle—from a dreaded dues-paying to a lofty reward—many actors are just going ahead and behaving as if they are ready-made serious artists who can strip if they want. You may think no one will be fooled, but Sharon Stone successfully uncrossed her legs into a sexy role in the Martin Scorsese movie *Casino*, beating out both the more established Melanie Griffith and the more "experienced" former porn star Traci Lords. Screen nudity doesn't just pay the rent, it clinches the deal.

Aside from the inevitable gnashing of teeth and beating of breasts over gray areas of morality, propriety, artistic license, and taste, the fact is that big-name screen nudity is here, it's in your face, and it's a phenomenon that bears examining.

It's no secret that sex sells, and movies are commodities just like cars, toothpaste, and plumbing supplies, all of which can be moved more easily off the shelves when an underclad body is draped over them. A diet drink takes on special appeal when a "construction worker" hunk removes his shirt and drinks one for a bunch of ogling career women. With high-profile models posing nude for antifur posters, sex even sells politics.

So, it's no surprise to anyone that sex sells movies. Celebrity skin is a natural area of interest for a society that avidly consumes every detail about the lives of its favorite stars. In this

Mexican hunk Ramon Novarro displays his chariot of fur in the 1926 silent epic *Ben-Hur;* his pubic region is only slightly airbrushed in this revealing publicity photo.

Photo courtesy of Photofest

Frank Currier and Ramon
Novarro return triumphantly
amid a sea of bare breasts in
1926's *Ben-Hur*; its opulence
and $4 million price tag were
more alarming at the time
than the nudity, a silent-film
staple.

Photo courtesy of Photofest

Even a petal-strewn bath can-
not conceal the charms of
Myrna Loy, a tourist in Egypt in
The Barbarian (1933), with
Ramon Novarro as her persis-
tent Arab guide.

Photo courtesy of Photofest

culture of celebrity, actors on the big screen seem so close, so intimate, that the audience feels they are not just watching them, but truly getting to know them. We refer to "Julia" and "Arnold" familiarly by their first names. We know who "Julia" has dated and broken up with, and how "Arnold" has mapped his career. The media saturates us with personality profiles, behind-the-scenes interviews, gossip, speculation, and photos. And now we know what "Julia" and "Arnold" (and everyone else in this book) looks like naked, down to the last mole and imperfection—which is something we can't say about almost

anyone else in the world except our mates. As Ted Danson once remarked, "People want to hug TV stars. They want to fuck movie stars."

Big-screen nudity satisfies our curiosity about celebrity bodies and also provides a sweet, private turn-on. They didn't call it *Basic Instinct* for nothing.

Movies need to be sold to a demanding audience. To that end, they employ the most highly visible, sexy, and attractive stars they can afford. Marketers launch campaigns that are organized with military precision. And the stars themselves have increasingly become the willing soldiers who march into battle, peeling off their underthings right and left to give their movies the sizzle that will make them victorious at the box office. Celebrity nudity not only sells movies, it sells the celebrities themselves.

Screen nudity wasn't invented by the current crop of exhibitionistic hardbodies. It wasn't even invented back when *Midnight Cowboy*, now considered a minor classic, got the first X rating by the Motion Picture Association of America (MPAA) in 1969 for its seedy depiction of male hustling.

Screen nudity has always been with us, not only in the parallel development of the porn industry, but in major Hollywood movies. A milestone was in 1961 when Natalie Wood became the first star in a major Hollywood feature to appear nude. She ran down the hall on her way to a nervous breakdown in *Splendor in the Grass*, a scene that hit the bricks at the firm request of the Legion of Decency.

People look back with affection on the chaste movies of yesteryear, but their memories are selective. No, you might not have noticed Clark Gable's privates, but that doesn't mean he wasn't appearing in salacious material. He watched Jean Harlow bathe nude in a barrel in *Red Dust* (1932), and he put the smile on Vivien Leigh's face in *Gone With the Wind* (1939) by hauling her up that staircase and raping her off-camera. Before the Production Code clamped down on Mae West in the thirties, contract players like Bette Davis, Barbara Stanwyck, and Joan Blondell were playing hookers, being abused, having illicit sex, and wearing scanty peekaboo outfits. Lissome young flapper Joan Crawford appeared nude in stag films in the twenties, still photos of which are still making the rounds. Tarzan and Jane were romp-

If you look closely, you'll see those aren't just forest tendrils curling out of Johnny Weissmuller's loincloth. The Legion of Decency cracked down on the former Olympic swimmer's *Tarzan* series, demanding more chaste tree-top accommodations for jungle playmate Maureen O'Sullivan.

Photo courtesy of Photofest

Jean Harlow lived fast and died young at age twenty-six, after thrilling moviegoers with her frank sexual expression and totally see-through gowns. What she spent to dye her hair platinum blond, she saved on panties, which she never wore.

ing in the jungle until the Legion of Decency snipped a nude bathing scene in 1934 between Johnny Weissmuller and Maureen O'Sullivan's stand-in and forced the unmarried couple to sleep more decorously in their tree house (thus virtually ruining the series). Victor Mature in a loincloth was billed in *One Million B.C.* (1940) as "a beautiful hunk of man." In 1944, while making *Lifeboat*, Tallulah Bankhead's insistence on stepping on and off the boat without wearing any underwear prompted director Alfred Hitchcock to quip that the problem should be addressed by "either hairdressing or makeup."

There's nothing Drew Barrymore shows today that wasn't seen back in 1933, the year fifteen-year-old Hedy Kiesler—later to be known as Hedy Lamarr—did the naked backstroke in *Ecstasy*, a Czech movie in which she cheerfully has a baby who resulted from her illicit (and explicit) lovemaking with a roadway engineer on her wedding night to another man. The movie was heralded as "the most whispered about film in the world" and "the stark naked truth of a woman's desire for love," but don't let that fool you— just as sex has been around since Adam and Eve, so have strategic marketing campaigns.

Today, actors of both sexes know which side their bread is buttered on. Former models like Kim Basinger, Demi Moore, and Phoebe Cates deliberately used their bodies to jump-start their acting careers. The Baldwin brothers seem locked in a sibling rivalry of sex appeal, each one taking successively more provocative roles to showcase his wares. Harvey Keitel, the unlikely poster boy for full-frontal nudity, whips it out only for the sake of art, but that's "art" defined broadly.

With so much being revealed, it's no wonder that word has trickled in from Hollywood as to who has the biggest member. Even *Spy* magazine has published lists with the usual suspects, like Willem Dafoe, James Woods, and Bruce Willis. Not surprisingly, the host with the most is usually the one out there preening like a peacock, which puts the shy guys in the default category—if Patrick Swayze shows his pecs but not his pecker, does that mean he has something to hide? One big-time action hunk is known derisively in Hollywood as "Princess Meat"; you'll never see him below the waist for love or money, and he's not a good enough actor to see him there for the sake of art.

So, it's not just a career move or a marketing technique that brings out the breast in some of these stars. There's an ego thing, too; there's an urge to immortalize their naked images on celluloid while still young and gorgeous the way they immortalized their handprints in the cement of Mann's Chinese Theater.

In the old days of

....
Mae West in her first starring role, 1933's *She Done Him Wrong*, invites a young Cary Grant to come up and see her sometime, the better to do him right. The Hays Code was instituted largely because of West's salty sexual one-liners.
....

the studio system, starlets were forced to endure the "casting couch" system of testing for a job. Today, Sharon Stone volunteers to do without the "crotch patch" that would separate her by a hair from Michael Douglas; Jamie Lee Curtis rues that the hottest part of her thonged striptease for Arnold Schwarzenegger wound up on the cutting-room floor; Melanie Griffith studies up for a role by getting her breasts enlarged; Goldie Hawn appears in a suspicious number of scenes that necessitate close-ups of her tattooed butt; Dana Delany throws herself into the role of dominatrix in order to change her good-girl image.

The men are no less eager to glorify their bodies in the interests of their careers. Richard Gere has happily led the way as a pioneer in breaking the male full-frontal taboo; Sylvester Stallone takes a cue from Demi Moore and poses completely nude on the cover of *Vanity Fair*; Michael Douglas specializes in movies where females devour his body and then try to bring him down; Bruce Willis proudly foregoes a body double so that Jane March can go down on him underwater; it was Eric

Theda Bara, that exotic gal with the name-change (from Theodosia Goodman) from Cincinnati, is a dandy in asps for 1917's Cleopatra.

Photo courtesy of Photofest

Stoltz's bright idea to let his penis do the acting in a dream sequence when the script didn't originally call for it; director Kevin Costner planned and executed a lingering shot of the Costner caboose in widescreen.

If you think all this naked posturing doesn't take talent, think again. A good actor makes the difficult look simple, and this is no less true for nude scenes. Naked on a set, actors are at their most vulnerable, at the mercy of the director, cinematographer, and even the screenwriter. A hot actress can easily be made to look grotesque (which has happened to Sean Young and Isabella Rossellini), while someone you might ordinarily think of as repulsive (that would be Mickey Rourke again) can carry a sex movie on his ability to get across a certain charisma. Careers can rise and fall on a sex scene—do we want to see k. d. lang naked again? Probably not. But Theresa Russell's body hasn't worn out its welcome even if she has.

There's no denying the sensual and voyeuristic pleasures—not to mention the simple curiosity factor—of seeing celebrities prance about in the nude. But it is also interesting to consider how their total exposure has aided and abetted their careers, played into the public's fantasies about them, changed the nature of how movies are marketed today, and helped to

Hard as it is to believe today, the popular Rock Hudson–Doris Day pairings were considered risqué for their time. In 1964's *Send Me No Flowers,* Hudson tries to unload wife Day on another man, the gay subtext of which was ferreted out by the enterprising pseudodocumentary *Rock Hudson's Home Movies* (1993), which reexamined Hudson's career in light of his homosexuality.

Sylvia Miles is still one sexy broad—or so she claims as she out-hustles hustler Jon Voight in *Midnight Cowboy*, the first mainstream movie to get an **X** under the new ratings system in 1969.

Photo courtesy of Photofest

define movies both worthy and worthless.

Here then are seventy-five stars (more if you count the hundreds of photos we have included) who have tied their fortunes to their bodies. How have they fared?

Bare Essentials

NUDE SCENES THAT HELPED DEFINE A CAREER

Kim Basinger

Bringing Out the Eros in Venetian Blinds

Former model and frequent *Playboy* exhibitionist Kim Basinger may well prefer to be remembered for her acting. But who is she kidding? Do we think of Kim and think *Nadine*? *Fool for Love*? Or do we think of the love slave of *9½ Weeks*, driven to near suicide by her uncontrollable compulsion to satisfy MICKEY ROURKE's every sick sexual whim?

9½ Weeks (1986) may be a sublimely stupid movie; few would argue the point. But it is also sublimely memorable, thanks in part to Basinger's portrayal of a masochistic career woman—bright enough to run an art gallery, but too dumb (and too busy unbuttoning) to look closely at her mysterious new boyfriend and see the warning signs, of which there are many. Even the set designer was sending up a flare by installing Rourke in a psychotically monochromatic apartment. At an amusement park, Rourke leaves Basinger stranded

Shrink Richard Gere gets his patient's sister, Basinger, off the couch and into bed in *Final Analysis*.

atop a Ferris wheel, where she discovers that abandonment and rejection are her secret turn-ons. The meaner he is, the more she bends to his will. He makes her dress as a man, commit petty larceny, endure a threesome, and crawl on the floor picking up dollar bills in her mouth (at least in the steamier European version). Isn't it romantic?

Basinger brings her body and pout to the role, but little else (although she later boasted it was her best work, that there were many more hours where that came from left on the cutting-room floor). Her acting skills can't make sense of the ending, where she is able to walk away from the sadist only once she realizes that she is willing to lay down her life for him. To understand her motivation in that scene after nine and one-half weeks of abuse, you'd have to read the book on which the movie is based.

The *New York Times* reported that Rourke and director Adrian Lyne (*Fatal Attraction*) conspired to make Basinger feel as awful off the set as on it, one of those "method" methods to make the actor become one with the character. It must have worked, because Basinger was bruised by the experience and has spent years overcompensating. *Premiere* magazine catalogued her contractual need for cases of Evian water with which to wash her lustrous locks and a personal assistant to protect her fair skin with a parasol during sunny shoots. On the set of *The Marrying Man*, she is alleged to have changed Neil Simon's script because she didn't think Simon knew how to write comedy. *Hellooo!*

Basinger, born in Athens, Georgia, on December 8, 1953, was a Breck Girl turned model who went to Hollywood determined to forge a career as the biggest blond bombshell since Marilyn Monroe. She was perfectly willing to take dumb-blonde roles, with Burt Reynolds in *The Man Who Loved Women* (1983) and with RICHARD GERE, who drags her handcuffed through the bayou in *No Mercy* (1986). On-screen, she seems like a woman crying out for either abuse or protection; her fans like it either way. "There's a quality she has that makes you care about her,"

....

(Opposite) Kim Basinger composes herself against arty lighting for the venetian-blind striptease of 9½ Weeks.

....

says Gere of his costar, adding that keeping the two of them handcuffed through
most of the movie was "provocative"
enough that they didn't need to take their
clothes off.

Interestingly, one cinematographer
explained Basinger's appeal as a function
of the downy fuzz on her fair face, which
catches and diffuses the light to make her
look dewy.

Basinger, who purposely posed for
Playboy to give her career a boost, made a
few unmemorable movies before she was
"discovered" as the Bond girl Domino in
Never Say Never Again (1983). There she
played a virtual prisoner of evil Klaus
Maria Brandauer, forced to dance alone
under surveillance cameras until rescued
by Sean Connery, who earlier gives her a
deeply penetrating massage.

Dancing for those surveillance cameras must be where Basinger caught the
voyeur bug, because in *9½ Weeks*, one of
her most memorable scenes involves a
pornographic dance for voyeur Rourke.
She wears a white slip and gyrates against
a stylishly minimalist background. Rarely
have venetian blinds been so closely identified with sex—which, come to think of
it, is probably a good thing.

Sex with common household items
did not stop there. In the famous kitchen
scene, Rourke blindfolds Basinger and
arouses her senses and taste buds by forc-

ing her to taste tidbits both nice and nasty out of the refrigerator. The fact that you can smell and thus anticipate a food before tasting it was not taken into account, probably because a blindfold has more erotic potential than a clothespin on the nose.

Those who appreciated Basinger for her physical virtues had to make do with the occasional breast, as in 1992's *Final Analysis*, when she makes love with shrink Richard Gere, until *The Getaway* in 1994 (available in two video versions), when she and real-life husband ALEC BALDWIN go at it with a vengeance. In this remake of the Steve McQueen–Ali MacGraw movie, Basinger plays Baldwin's moll, and when he gets out of prison, he's starved for attention. She gives it to him. He gives it back to her. The lighting is as dim as her character was in *Cool World* (1992), when she played a pneumatic cartoon character named Holli Would, who comes to life after having sex with

Basinger clings to the fleshy midriff of mysterious new boyfriend Mickey Rourke, who teaches her the pleasures of total sexual obedience in 9½ Weeks.

the cartoonist (Gabriel Byrne) who drew her.

Basinger, the first girl in the Batcave (although she wasn't asked to return for *Batman Returns*), has done some interesting things with her millions. She bought a town in her home state of Georgia, then declared bankruptcy after she was fined $8.9 million for skipping out of the lead in *Boxing Helena* (1993). She might have felt that playing a woman whose limbs are surgically removed by the man who is obsessed with her would not further her career, but her rationale for quitting, as she told the court, was her sudden, mid-career objection to doing nude scenes. "The more flesh you show, the higher up the ladder you go," she complained of the demands the business makes on the prettiest.

Instead, she made the equally dismal *The Real McCoy*, which only goes to prove the irony of things. The only part of her form that we see is its outline when she wears a bodysuit to rob banks (and from that distance it could easily be a body double). If only Basinger had chosen more wisely, done more vulnerable sex movies like *9½ Weeks*, she might have become the new Marilyn after all. Instead, she'll have to live with having turned down *Basic Instinct* and ending up in *Cool World*.

FILMOGRAPHY

Hard Country, 1981
Mother Lode, 1982
The Man Who Loved Women, 1983
Never Say Never Again, 1983
The Natural, 1984
Fool for Love, 1985
9½ Weeks, 1986
No Mercy, 1986
Blind Date, 1987
Nadine, 1987
My Stepmother Is an Alien, 1988
Batman, 1989
The Marrying Man, 1991
Cool World, 1992
Final Analysis, 1992
The Real McCoy, 1993
Wayne's World 2, 1993
The Getaway, 1994
Prêt-à-Porter, 1995

Jennifer Beals
What a Feeling

I n *Flashdance,* Jennifer Beals introduced the nation to two new fashion crazes—wearing torn sweatshirts and nothing else around the house, and lubriciously massaging your own thighs.

Except those weren't Jennifer's own thighs she was massaging. After *Flashdance* became a surprise 1983 hit, catapulting the Chicago-born Yale student (then twenty years old) to a stardom her career hasn't matched since, it was revealed that much of the exotic dance and sweaty warm-up scenes were courtesy of Marine Jahan, a body double and trained dancer, who later resented not getting any credit.

Not that Beals had anything to hide. After a career interrupted to finish school and then set back by appearing with Sting (and yet another body double) in *The Bride* (1986), she later displayed her own wares in movies such as *Vampire's Kiss* (1989) and *Blood and Concrete* (1991). She was most truly herself in the Italian *Caro Diario* (1994), in which director and monologuist

Nanni Moretti babbles on about wanting to meet the star of *Flashdance* and then happens to run into her on a street in Rome. (It's her own body—clothed, of course—and she speaks her own Italian.)

In *Flashdance*—technically her second movie after a bit role as a terrorized high schooler in *My Bodyguard* (1980)—the honey-skinned, doe-eyed Beals played Alex, welder by day, exotic dancer by night, and all-around dreamer, whose secret ambition

FILMOGRAPHY

My Bodyguard, 1980
Flashdance, 1983
The Bride, 1985
La Partita, 1988
Split Decisions, 1988
Vampire's Kiss, 1988
Sons, 1989
Docteur M. (Club Extinction), 1990
The Gamble, 1990
Blood and Concrete, a Love Story,
1991
In the Soup, 1992
Day of Atonement, 1993
Caro diario, 1994
Mrs. Parker and the Vicious Circle,
1994
Four Rooms, 1995

is to chuck the blowtorch and shuck the pasties for a career in toeshoes.

Alex begins dating her handsome welding boss after he catches her midnight show, where she dreams up such dance numbers as the infamous one in which she leans back in a chair, pulls a string, and gets doused with a bucket of water. This is followed by a frenzy of backlit hair-tossing, with director Adrian Lyne using the glossy, eye-catching film techniques he had learned in England when making television commercials.

The neatest trick in *Flashdance* is how Alex wiggles out of her underclothes while still wearing that sweatshirt, à la ANN-MARGRET in *Bye Bye Birdie*. It leaves the impression that we've seen Beals unmasked, when in fact it would be two more years before the wet-nightgown scene in *The Bride*, performed without the body double whose lower torso fills in for Beals earlier in that same movie.

As Beals pursues her adult career, she is trying new things. She sings in *Blood and Concrete* (1991), a movie in which she plays a suicidal nymphomaniac. She plays Robert Benchley's very traditional suburban wife in Alan Rudolph's *Mrs. Parker and the Vicious Circle* (1994), a teetotaler and homemaker so conservative she can't understand Dorothy Parker's one-liners, and certainly wouldn't be caught dead rubbing her thighs. And in *Four Rooms* (1995), in a segment directed by her husband, Alexandre Rockwell, she is a cheating wife tied to a chair. Rockwell wrote that segment and cast Beals, who apparently doesn't mind being tied up when it's all in the family.

Annette Bening

Paying Rent on the Barter Plan

Annette Bening made good out of playing bad. In *Valmont* (1989), only her second film, she reprised Glenn Close's Marquise de Merteuil, whose unholy delight in decadent sexual gamesmanship causes the ruination of everyone around her in eighteenth-century France—including herself. No one saw *Valmont,* and everyone saw Close in *Dangerous Liaisons*, so it was lucky for Bening that *Liaisons* director Stephen Frears rescued her from possible obscurity.

Frears had actually auditioned Bening for his movie before he cast Close. To make it up to her, he corralled her wanton sexuality in *The Grifters* (1990) for the role of Myra Langtry, one of an unholy triumvirate of con artists.

Myra is a tall drink of water rather short on morals and, often, clothing. She is out to outswindle her hustler lover (John Cusack) and his equally proficient hustler mom (Anjelica Huston), who replaced Bening's clone, MELANIE GRIFFITH, in this adaptation of Jim Thompson's tough, noir novel.

Myra is a woman who cares about her work, which consists of fleecing others on the grand scale. She uses everything at her disposal to advance her career—particularly her body. It is telling that of the times we see her naked, one is with the landlord to whom she pays rent in a sexual barter arrangement, the other is when she is lying dead in the morgue.

"I remembered at first when people would ask me about doing nude scenes, I'd say, well, it speaks for itself. But I realized I'd have to actually talk about it, because so many people ask," says Bening, drawing a deep breath before plunging in. "When I read the script, there was a certain wildness and outrageousness to Myra that I thought was absolutely true. So, I never looked

....

In *The Grifters*, con artist Bening trades sexual favors for the rent.

....

at it and thought that I wanted to do the part but not the nudity. So, my question was whether I wanted to do the whole thing. I thought about it, and I spoke to Stephen Frears about it, deciding about it, about the specifics of those scenes. I also liked it because it was comedic. It was not lovemaking, a passionate scene or something. The context it was in, I felt comfortable with it. So, just in very simple terms, those are the reasons I felt that it was no big deal."

Working on *Valmont* earlier in Prague had a salutary effect as well. "Being in Europe, among European attitudes, did have an influence on me, in terms of nudity and the human body. It's much more accepted over there, it's not like this big thing. We're still very puritanical here about it. But there it was no big deal. Would I do scenes like that again? I don't know. Maybe, maybe not."

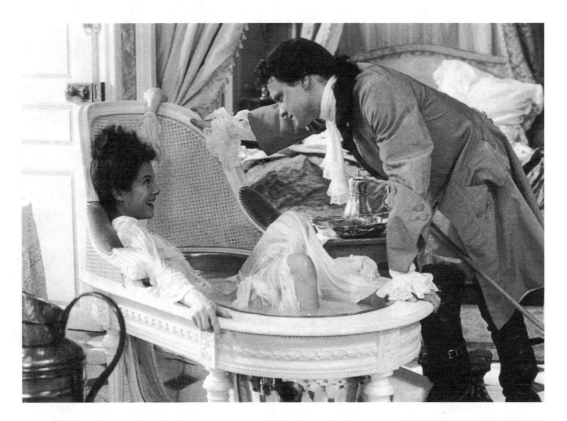

Not only nude scenes, but costumes can give an actress a sense of her character's physicality. "It's one of the fun things about acting, to change the way you appear and dress. It has a tremendous influence on your inner life. In *The Grifters*, I wore a lot of spandex."

With the double-whammy of *Valmont* and *The Grifters*, Bening developed a fast reputation for playing sexually avaricious females, and she played them with obvious relish and delight, not with the modicum of moral reserve that some actresses add so that the audience can feel a little sorry for the character. She managed to upstage MERYL STREEP—an actress she admits intimidated her—in a tiny supporting role in *Postcards From the Edge* as a love rival for the callow Dennis Quaid. While walking and suggestively sucking a lollipop, she reveals quite casually to the crest-

Annette Bening's come-hither look to Colin Firth travels from her smile right down to her legs in *Valmont*, in which she enthusiastically wrecks the morals and love lives of those around her.

Photo courtesy of Photofest

Actress turned gun-moll Bening encourages soon-to-be lover (both on- and off-screen) Warren Beatty to go outside and jerk himself a soda in *Bugsy*.

fallen Streep that she has also slept with Quaid, and confirms his usual pickup line.

That led to playing the sultry mob moll, Virginia Hill, in *Bugsy* (1991), the movie on which she met future husband (and until then famous bachelor) Warren Beatty. "Whyn't ya go outside and jerk yourself a soda?" she taunts Beatty, who plays mobster and early Las Vegas visionary Bugsy Siegel.

After eavesdropping on a furious Bugsy reducing a fellow criminal to jelly, Virginia develops a truly romantic pity for him and showers him with kisses while his mouth is full at dinner; they drop to the floor to make love and the rest is history, or at least the history of Vegas.

The actress LAURA DERN wasn't too crazy about that scene. Dern told *Movieline*: "*Bugsy* really annoyed me when Annette Bening got off on Warren Beatty making that guy bark like a dog, there's just no reason for that." *Movieline* helpfully relayed this to Bening, who retorted: "Maybe it's a politically incorrect thing for a woman, but I think it's human."

Although the actress doesn't feel taken advantage of in those early nude scenes, she does acknowledge the double standard of filmdom. "Having played opposite [ROBERT] DE NIRO (*Guilty by Suspicion*) and Harrison (Ford) (*Regarding Henry*), and Warren, I think there is definitely more tolerance for a man getting older than for a woman," she says. "It's not always true, and there are a

lot of exceptions to that, but it definitely exists, that double standard. It's part of our culture right now. I live in Los Angeles, and there's that whole thing about plastic surgery and women aging and the way that women are supposed to feel about themselves."

Marriage to Beatty and motherhood have changed the tide of Bening's career. When she first became pregnant, she ceded the role of Catwoman in *Batman Returns* (1992) to MICHELLE PFEIFFER. Her second pregnancy cost her *Disclosure* (1994), which went to DEMI MOORE. She finally returned to films opposite her husband in *Love Affair* (1994), the second remake of the romantic chestnut about star-crossed lovers who were meant to be together despite previous engagements and that little traffic accident. Much of the dialogue between Bening and Beatty reflects their own circumstance: "You know, I've never been faithful to anyone in my whole life," he tells her. That doesn't spoil her appetite.

Love Affair celebrated the possibilities of monogamy and the possibilities for Bening to be sexy on-screen without having to peel off the spandex—but too few cared and the movie died at the box office. Although she missed her opportunity with *Disclosure* to sexually harass MICHAEL DOUGLAS, she replaced Emma Thompson in order to romance Douglas in the very clothed comedy *The American President* (1995).

FILMOGRAPHY

The Great Outdoors, 1987
Valmont, 1990
Postcards From the Edge, 1990
The Grifters, 1990
Guilty by Suspicion, 1991
Regarding Henry, 1991
Bugsy, 1991
Love Affair, 1994
The American President, 1995

Jacqueline Bisset
Scuba-Dooba-Doo

If Jacques Cousteau had offered the sights on display in the scuba-diving drama *The Deep* (1977), oceanography might have become as glamorous as undercover work.

In *The Deep*, the principal sight is Bisset in a wet T-shirt. It wasn't quite as popular as Farrah Fawcett's hair that same year, but it sold posters and a so-so movie. Bisset plays Gail Berke, vacationing in Bermuda with her husband (NICK NOLTE). They scuba-dive and dredge up more than pretty shells—they find treasure, drugs, and trouble aplenty.

With her upper-crust accent and air of cool intelligence, the British-born Jacqueline Fraser-Bisset may have discarded various articles of underwear during her film career, but she always managed to lend her projects a certain class. (No wonder she was cast in 1983's *Class* as the mother who seduces her son's

....

Jackie Bisset puts a dramatic spin on the wet T-shirt genre in *The Deep*.

....

FILMOGRAPY

The Knack...and How to Get It, 1965
Cul-de-Sac, 1966
The Cape Town Affair, 1967
Casino Royale, 1967
Two for the Road, 1967
Bullitt, 1968
The Detective, 1968
The Sweet Ride, 1968
The First Time, 1969
Airport, 1970
The Grasshopper, 1970
The Mephisto Waltz, 1970
Believe in Me, 1971
Secrets, 1971
The Life and Times of Judge Roy Bean, 1972
Stand Up and Be Counted, 1972
Day for Night, 1973
The Thief Who Came to Dinner, 1973
Le Magnifique, 1974
Murder on the Orient Express, 1974
Der Richter and sein Henker, 1975
La Donna della Domenica, 1976
St. Ives, 1976
The Deep, 1977
The Greek Tycoon, 1978
Who Is Killing the Great Chefs of Europe?, 1978
Amo non amo, 1979
When Time Ran Out, 1980
Rich and Famous, 1981
Inchon, 1982
Class, 1983
Notes From Under the Volcano, 1984
Observations Under the Volcano, 1984
Under the Volcano, 1984
High Season, 1987
La Maison de Jade, 1988
Scenes From the Class Struggle in Beverly Hills, 1989
Wild Orchid, 1990
The Maid, 1990

college roommate.)Born September 13, 1944, the model turned actress's major career accomplishment has been modeling herself on film. Her sex scenes invariably play off her ladylike demeanor, regal bearing, and the statuesque forthrightness that makes her seem the seducer. Fans may overlook her fine work in Francois Truffaut's *Day for Night* (1973) and John Huston's *Under the Volcano* (1984), but they never forget Jackie scuba-diving in that sheer T-shirt.

(Above) Bisset back on dry land, but still recognizable.

Photo courtesy of Albert Ferreira/DMI

Phoebe Cates

Pooled Resources

Phoebe Cates only appears topless in Judge Reinhold's fantasy in *Fast Times at Ridgemont High* (1982), but evidently he is not alone in dreaming.

The gorgeous, chipmunk-cheeked former teen model, the epitome of adorableness, was educated in dance at Juilliard and the Professional Children's School in her hometown of New York City. An early career switch to acting seemed appropriate, considering that her father is the producer-director Joseph Cates and her uncle, director Gilbert Cates.

In her first two movies, the *Blue Lagoon* ripoff *Paradise* (1982) and the high school vignette movie *Fast Times at Ridgemont High*, Cates stripped at the drop of a bikini. In *Fast Times*, Reinhold daydreams about his sister's friends splashing about in the backyard pool, imagining Linda Barrett (Cates) rising up out of the water in slo-mo, topless and fairly oozing with desire. In reality, Linda is thoroughly grossed out when she stumbles upon Reinhold in the bathroom masturbating to his fantasies. Her rejection of him is indicative

FILMOGRAPHY

Paradise, 1982
Fast Times at Ridgemont High, 1982
Private School, 1983
Gremlins, 1984
Date With an Angel, 1987
Bright Lights, Big City, 1988
Shag, 1988
Heart of Dixie, 1989
Gremlins 2: The New Batch, 1990
I Love You to Death, 1990
Drop Dead Fred, 1991
Bodies, Rest and Motion, 1993
My Life's in Turnaround, 1994
Princess Caraboo, 1994

of his comic downward spiral, which includes losing the "coveted" job of manager of a fast-food joint at the mall.

Another memorable scene involves a carrot, which Cates borrows from her high school lunchroom tray in order to give pal JENNIFER JASON LEIGH an object lesson in the techniques of oral sex—much to the approval of the boys at an adjacent table. In *Paradise*, made that same year, she showered as nature intended—under a waterfall.

Now married to actor Kevin Kline, Cates is a mother and wife, but still irresistibly cute as a button opposite him in *Princess Caraboo* (1994) as a winningly mysterious woman who has been embraced by a small English town as a possibly blue-blooded Javanese princess. Kline, as the arrogant Greek butler Frixos, is not fooled. *"I know you are a fake and I have speet in your soup!"* he hisses as he serves her dinner. John Lithgow plays a stammering academic who is thoroughly unnerved while attempting to trace a royal tattoo up the lady's thigh to parts unknown.

Princess Caraboo wasn't the first time Cates was paired with her husband. In an unbilled cameo in *I Love You to Death* (1990), she plays one of hubby's one-night stands. On television, Cates has kept her clothes on, but she still knows how to create a scene, as she did in the miniseries *Lace* (1984) when she bellowed, *"Which one of you bitches is my mother?"*

Not since acting in teen trifles has Cates unbuttoned, but she is still remembered by many viewers—as is evidenced by the thunderous wolf whistles she receives when she appears on talk shows—the way Judge Reinhold once thought of her.

(Opposite) Phoebe Cates (*left*) takes a backyard dip with Jennifer Jason Leigh while Judge Reinhold is secretly getting off on the fantasy of seeing her topless in *Fast Times at Ridgemont High*.

Laura Dern

Taking a Walk on the Wild at Heart Side

Laura Dern makes dirty sex seem sweet. She played the small-town virginal antidote to ISABELLA ROSSELLINI in 1986's *Blue Velvet* for director David Lynch. As she is the opposite of the bosomy blondes who typically populate Lynch's movies, it means he hired her on the strength of her acting, while still having faith in her physicality. Four years later, Lynch had Dern explore that wild side he had spied in *Wild at Heart*.

"Laura is a tidbit," said the director of casting this tall, initially shy and gangly actress as a seething mass of Southern sexuality.

In *Wild at Heart*, Dern is Lula, the exuberantly physical girlfriend of Nicolas Cage. She is topless over the course of any number of lengthy, explicit sexual encounters, including one which the *Bare Facts Video Guide* praises for its "great moaning."

"Laura is the kind of person who is genuinely likable," says Cage of his costar. "She's fun to be around, and you like being with her. The last thing you want to do on a movie set is be with someone you can't stand and jump into bed and wrestle with them. Just the sheer fact that she's such a sweet personality made it easier."

Making it easier still was the camaraderie that developed between Dern and Cage thanks to a novel suggestion by Laura's real-life dad, actor Bruce Dern. "He thought it would be a good idea to spend some time together," says Cage, who took Laura on a twenty-four hour, get-acquainted road trip to Las Vegas to prepare for their roles.

"We cultivated enough trust on that trip so we could let the more subtle aspects of sex come through," says Cage. "The sex in the movie is totally my favorite thing about the film, because it's so pure, and when I watch it, I don't feel that I'm spying on these people, I feel like I'm celebrating it with them. Sex has been exploited and presented in the most tacky ways in the past. Here, it may be violent at times, but it's thoughtful, meaningful, and shows that sex is a good thing, that it's okay for people in love to have radical sex. It should be celebrated, not shunned or feared."

Wild at Heart nearly got a life-threatening X rating, so a few scenes were trimmed. "I said please don't touch the sensual stuff," says Cage. "There are moments when the sex stops, and there's a thought, one of those resting things that happens during sex, and then it starts up again. It just felt very pure."

Dern had previously played an adolescent, whose body is

Nubile teenager Laura Dern's body sends out signals her emotions can't handle in *Smooth Talk.*

FILMOGRAPHY

White Lightning, 1973
Alice Doesn't Live Here Anymore, 1974
Foxes, 1980
Ladies and Gentlemen, The Fabulous Stains, 1982
Teachers, 1984
Mask, 1985
Smooth Talk, 1985
Blue Velvet, 1986
Sister, Sister, 1987
Haunted Summer, 1988
Fat Man and Little Boy, 1989
Wild at Heart, 1990
Rambling Rose, 1991
Jurassic Park, 1993
A Perfect World, 1993

way ahead of her emotions, in *Smooth Talk* (1985). There, her unconsciously provocative sexuality entices the dangerous Treat Williams, who rapes her. After making *Wild at Heart,* Dern said she was finally liberated personally and professionally—indeed, as she said this, she practically writhed in her chair with pleasure at her own newly discovered physicality. "The crew was so gracious and protective," she said. "A crew that's harsh and makes little jokes behind your back while you're naked—I wouldn't be able to open up in front of people like that."

She won a Best Actress Oscar nomination as the sexually rapacious free spirit who comes to stay with Robert Duvall and Diane Ladd in *Rambling Rose* (1991). (Ladd, her real-life mother, also received an Oscar nomination that year for Supporting Actress.) The first shot of Dern shows the light streaming through her deceptively innocent sundress. Before long, her character has seduced nearly every male within miles, including her host. Local boys howl outside her window like cats in heat.

In *Jurassic Park* (1993), Dern plays a rather dry paleontologist who sifts through dinosaur dung with gusto. But now that audiences know Dern is a "tidbit," it's hard to believe she'll be spending much screen time in a lab coat.

Body and emotions are merged and ready by the time Dern goes on the road with Nicolas Cage in *Wild at Heart*.

Susan Sarandon

A Twist of Lemon

When you think of Susan Sarandon, you think of rescuing Haitian boat people. You think of Thelma and Louise cruising down the highways of America. You think of lemons.

The Haitians are one of the political causes Sarandon and her outspoken companion, Tim Robbins, have espoused. *Thelma & Louise* is one of several movies that have kept the actress in the public eye as a strong-willed sex symbol long past the age when actresses are usually (and unfairly) put out to pasture.

The lemons are what she rubbed all over her breasts, arms, and hands in *Atlantic City* as Burt Lancaster watched covertly from a window across the way.

In Louis Malle's poignant 1981 Oscar-nominated movie, Sarandon is Sally, a woman who dreams of being a classy casino croupier and who bathes in lemon juice to remove the smell of oysters each night. The movie's blatant sensuality saw Sarandon nominated for Best Actress. Her breasts were dis-

Susan Sarandon sued unsuccessfully to prevent explicit *Pretty Baby* set photos from winding up in magazines. She was told that as she has participated in allowing the public to perceive her as a sex symbol, she had no right to object.

cussed with the detail of a post-doctoral thesis in every magazine on the newsstands. *Playboy* said she had "the celebrity breasts of the summer," leading Sarandon to worry "what was coming in the fall."

"Legally, I'm considered a sex symbol," Sarandon said after she lost a suit to stop *Pretty Baby* outtakes from appearing in magazines. "I was told the photos weren't damaging because that's who I am."

Sarandon was born Susan Tomaling on October 4, 1946, (she got the "Sarandon" from her ex-husband, actor Chris), and studied drama at Catholic University in Washington, D.C. Beginning with her full-frontal film debut in the bathtub in 1970's *Joe*, the former model has had many nude scenes in a career that, due to her intelligence and force of personality, never has been regarded as lightweight or merely decorative. She was frankly naked in another Malle film, *Pretty Baby* (1978), as the prostitute mother of BROOKE SHIELDS. She nibbled on Catherine Deneuve's nipple in the 1983 lesbian vampire film *The Hunger* (although Deneuve used a body double for several scenes), and she bared her soul and practically everything else to an appreciative James Spader in the May–December romance *White Palace* (1990).

"I think it's very hard to be naked in a scene and not be upstaged by your nipples," Sarandon told *Movieline*. "People don't even hear what you're saying for the first thirty seconds if you're standing there nude."

To Sarandon's credit, some of her sexiest scenes have had little or no nudity. While it's true that her feminist revolt against a patriarchal terrain in 1991's *Thelma & Louise* was made more palatable for politically timid viewers by the fact that Sarandon and Geena Davis staged this revolt braless, a more romantically salient image was that of KEVIN COSTNER painting baseball fan Sarandon's toes in *Bull Durham* (1988), the movie on which she met future companion Robbins.

There was also a great deal of fully clothed heat between Sarandon as an inquisitive housewife and the late Raul Julia as a

Susan Sarandon washes all over with lemon to get the smell of seafood off her in *Atlantic City*, with Burt Lancaster spying on her from across the way.

FILMOGRAPHY

Joe, 1970
The Front Page, 1974
Lovin' Molly, 1974
Dragonfly, 1975
The Great Waldo Pepper, 1975
The Rocky Horror Picture Show, 1975
Crash, 1976
The Great Smokey Roadblock, 1976
Checkered Flag or Crash, 1977
The Other Side of Midnight, 1977
King of the Gypsies, 1978
Pretty Baby, 1978
Something Short of Paradise, 1979
Loving Couples, 1980
Atlantic City, 1981
Tempest, 1982
The Hunger, 1983
The Buddy System, 1984
In Our Hands, 1984
Compromising Positions, 1985
The Witches of Eastwick, 1987
Bull Durham, 1988
Sweet Hearts Dance, 1988
The January Man, 1989
A Dry White Season, 1989
Through the Wire, 1990
White Palace, 1990
Thelma & Louise, 1991
Bob Roberts, 1992
Light Sleeper, 1992
The Player, 1992
Lorenzo's Oil, 1993
The Client, 1994
Little Women, 1994
Safe Passage, 1995
Dead Man Walking, 1995

police detective in *Compromising Positions* (1985), a movie in which the compromise was that Sarandon and Julia get their kicks from solving the murder of a dentist instead of from giving in to their mutual attraction.

Sarandon is a good example of how sexuality depends more on acting ability than centimeters of exposed flesh. In *The Client* (1994), for which she was nominated for an Oscar, she is a lawyer protecting a young boy, who has seen a little too much for his own good. The mob is after the kid, and so is arrogant district attorney Tommy Lee Jones. At the end, Sarandon and Jones are still sparring, Tracy–Hepburn style, when Sarandon reaches out to straighten the tie of her nemesis. Under the circumstances, the scene couldn't have been hotter if it had been brushed with lemon juice and broiled.

Christian Slater

"I Won't Do a Love Scene If It's Grotesque and Lewd."

A severe case of puppy love broke out in teen magazines everywhere when a fifteen-year-old named Christian Slater bared his tender tush for the screen in *The Name of the Rose* in 1986.

Today, adolescent girls (and their older sisters) are still baying at the moon whenever the Jack Nicholson sound-alike makes an appearance. One can even say that Slater's die-hard fans helped pull *Robin Hood: Prince of Thieves* out of the fire in 1991 for his small role as Will Scarlett, more of an audience contemporary than KEVIN COSTNER's somber, politically correct Robin Hood.

The New York-born teen idol made his film debut in the forgettable *The Legend of Billie Jean* in 1985, opposite Helen Slater (no relation), on whom Slater had a crush. It was while making this movie that he claims to have lost his virginity (although not, alas, to his namesake).

Then he costarred as investigative cleric Sean Connery's tonsured sidekick in *The Name of the Rose*, about monk murders in thirteenth-century Italy.

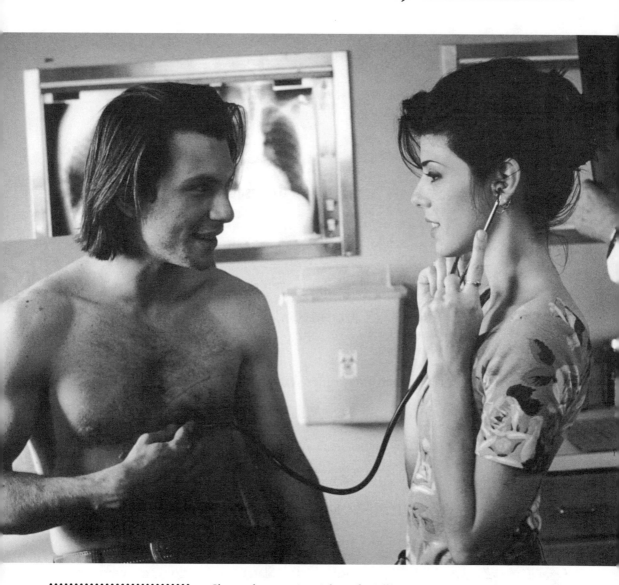

Marisa Tomei checks to see if there's a heart to go with the heavy breathing of Christian Slater in *Untamed Heart*.

Slater plays novice Adso of Melk, an innocent until a local peasant wench gets hold of him. "The actress in the scene [Valerina Vargas] guided me through," recalls Slater. "The love scenes were shot on a cold stone floor with dead fish lying around, not the most sexual thing at all. I don't like to be filmed while I'm making love. I won't do a love scene if it's grotesque and lewd and there's no point to it."

Well, he's still young.

Born August 18, 1969, in New York, Slater has become an acting fixture for his generation, in particular because of his role as a high school rebel in *Heathers* (1989), killing off anyone in his class he doesn't care for. He continued in a similar vein in 1990's *Pump Up the Volume* as an anonymous radio pirate deejay whose teen point of view and irreverence—he pretends to masturbate on the air—become a cause célèbre among the local high schoolers.

Mobsters, a 1991 flop, signaled Slater's move toward more adult roles, playing Lucky Luciano and again being assigned a brief sex scene. In 1994's *Interview With the Vampire*, he took over the role meant for the late River Phoenix as the curious journalist who succumbs to the power, glory, and finally, the wet kiss of the vampire—that last courtesy of fellow film hunk TOM CRUISE.

When Slater, possessed of a healthy sense of humor, is asked what he thinks made him stand out in *The Name of the Rose* despite his youth and inexperience, he replies simply: "My penis."

FILMOGRAPHY

The Legend of Billie Jean, 1985
The Name of the Rose, 1986
Twisted, 1985
Gleaming the Cube, 1988
Personal Choice, 1988
Tucker: The Man and His Dream, 1988
Heathers, 1989
The Wizard, 1989
Pump Up the Volume, 1990
Tales From the Darkside, The Movie, 1990
Young Guns II, 1990
Robin Hood: Prince of Thieves, 1991
Mobsters, 1991
Star Trek VI: The Undiscovered Country, 1991
Kuffs, 1992
Ferngully: The Last Rainforest (voice), 1992
Where the Day Takes You, 1992
Untamed Heart, 1993
True Romance, 1993
The Last Party, 1993
Interview With the Vampire, 1994
Amelia and the King of Plants, 1995
Murder in the First, 1995

Uma Thurman

Pushing the Ratings Envelope

Not many serious actresses can overcome being used as a nude writing desk. John Malkovich pens a letter to another love interest by leaning on teenage Uma Thurman's buttocks after deflowering her.

As Thurman has gone on to unleash the passions of many a male costar, her own were unleashed early in her career in *Dangerous Liaisons* (1988), director Stephen Frears's rendering of the 1782 novel about sexual debauchery among the bored upper classes in France.

Thurman, only eighteen herself at the time, played the virginal sixteen-year-old Cecile de Volanges, betrothed to a former lover of the scheming Marquise de Merteuil (Glenn Close). The Marquise enlists her equally unregenerate pal (Malkovich) to relieve Cecile of her virginity so as to punish the future groom, who believes his bride will be pure.

Cecile is properly horrified, ashamed, and distraught over her deflowering—for a few moments, anyway. Then she finds that she likes sex and sex

likes her, and the joke is that she can't get enough of it.

Thurman, the willowy former wife of *Dracula* star Gary Oldman, was born April 29, 1970, in Boston. She followed her debut in 1987's *Kiss Daddy Good Night* with three films released in 1988, *Dangerous Liaisons*, *Johnny Be Good*, and *The Adventures of Baron Munchausen*, where she was a spectacular (and spectacularly nude) *Venus de Milo* come to life.

A slender teen who casually disrobed, Thurman seemed very modern using one of the movies' oldest attention-getting devices. By the time she starred in 1990's *Henry and June*, Thurman in the buff was old news. Still, this creamily filmed Philip Kaufman movie about the writer Henry Miller (Fred Ward) and the lesbian affair between his wife, the bisexual former taxi dancer June (Thurman), and his moon-faced mistress, the erotic writer Anaïs Nin (Maria de Medeiros), earned *Henry and June* a curious place in cinema history—it was the first to carry a studio-sanctioned NC–17 rating.

Uma Thurman (*right*) in look-alike eyeliner for her lesbian scenes with Maria de Madeiros in *Henry and June*, the first studio film to carry an NC–17 rating.

When Thurman tested against Tom Hanks for the role of his mistress in *Bonfire of the Vanities*, she made Hanks perspire. He was so uncomfortable that Thurman lost the role to MELANIE GRIFFITH. She does something similar to ROBERT DE NIRO's character in *Mad Dog and Glory*, a role she did get. Here, she is tough-guy Bill Murray's concubine; Murray "gives" her to the meek De Niro as a thank-you for saving Murray's life. Thurman's endowments may not have been enough to secure a following for the movie, but her lengthy sofa make-out scene with De Niro prompts his character to worry whether he has done enough sit-ups to be worthy of her. He must have been worthy enough, because in real life the two carried on briefly after the movie wrapped. "Sometimes it's easier [to do nude scenes] if you don't know the person you're working with," she has said. But she hated the way her nude scenes were filmed in that movie, with the crew looking on and ogling her.

....

Robert De Niro may not have done enough sit-ups to justify receiving Thurman as a "gift" in *Mad Dog & Glory*, but the two wound up doing a little unwrapping off-screen as well.

....

In *Even Cowgirls Get the Blues* (made in 1993, but released after some emergency triage in 1994), Thurman is all thumbs as the hitch-hiking heroine of the Tom Robbins novel about lesbian cowgirls out West. The role may have been perfect for Thurman, whose slender, attenuated fingers and toes are all the rage among digit enthusiasts. But her nondescript love scenes with cowgirl Rain Phoenix and mountain dweller Noriyuki "Pat" Morita couldn't save this muddled Gus Van Sant bomb.

Thurman was more than redeemed by her laconically stylized and ultimately hilarious Oscar-nominated turn as a gangster's bored wife

in Quentin Tarantino's 1994 *Pulp Fiction.* It is the stuff of legend that a man was thrown out a high window for daring to give Thurman's character a foot massage. Later, she slinks around to the tune of "Girl, You'll Be a Woman Soon" as she and John Travolta anticipate a night of steamy infidelity. Their fire is doused when Thurman overdoses in a heart-pounding scene that sent one audience member into an insulin faint at the opening night of the 1994 New York Film Festival. Perhaps that is just Thurman's natural effect on viewers.

FILMOGRAPHY

Kiss Daddy Good Night, 1987
The Adventures of Baron
Munchausen, 1988
Dangerous Liaisons, 1988
Johnny Be Good, 1988
Henry and June, 1990
Where the Heart Is, 1990
Final Analysis, 1992
Jennifer 8, 1992
Mad Dog and Glory, 1993
Even Cowgirls Get the Blues, 1993
Pulp Fiction, 1994
Beautiful Girls, 1995

Kathleen Turner

Not Bad, Just Drawn That Way

What male and female audiences find sexy can be very different. For instance, women enjoy the scene in *Body Heat* (1981) when WILLIAM HURT breaks through the window of Kathleen Turner's home to get to her, because women like the idea of a man so inflamed with passion that he'll move heaven, earth, and a little plate glass to achieve his desire. And men like the scene in that same movie where Turner is prone on her heaving bed, with Hurt above her, because men like to see sex performed in various kama sutra positions.

Either way, audiences of both genders felt the heat in *Body Heat,* Turner's film debut after a career on daytime soaps. *Body Heat* was Lawrence Kasdan's update of the classic film noir *Double Indemnity* (1944), in which Barbara Stanwyck convinces the salivating insurance salesman Fred MacMurray to help her solve a little husband problem of hers. In *Body Heat,* bored rich wife Turner and loser lawyer Hurt meet cute when she says, "You're not too smart,

There's nothing between Kathleen Turner and her *Body Heat* except this flimsy night-gown, which is why William Hurt breaks through a window to get to her.

are you? I like that in a man."

Scenes of the husky-voiced Turner in a sheer silk negligee are enough to explain the errant behavior of the lustful lawyer, but Turner adds several R-rated flashes of skin to reinforce his character motivation.

Turner was born in Springfield, Missouri, on June 19, 1954. She attended Southwest Missouri State University, the University of Maryland, and London's Central School of Speech and Drama. *Body Heat* should have made her an overnight star, but it

FILMOGRAPHY

Body Heat, 1981
The Man With Two Brains, 1983
A Breed Apart, 1984
Crimes of Passion, 1984
Romancing the Stone, 1984
The Jewel of the Nile, 1985
Prizzi's Honor, 1985
Peggy Sue Got Married, 1986
Dear America, 1987
Julia and Julia, 1987
The Accidental Tourist, 1988
Switching Channels, 1988
Who Framed Roger Rabbit (voice),
1988
Tummy Trouble (voice; short),
1989
The War of the Roses, 1989
Rollercoaster Rabbit (voice; short),
1990
V. I. Warshawski, 1991
Undercover Blues, 1993
House of Cards, 1993
Serial Mom, 1994

wasn't until she teamed with Michael Douglas for the first of three action-comedy-romance pairings that she really clicked— *Romancing the Stone* in 1984.

Meanwhile, Turner laid claim to being Queen of Curves in Ken Russell's typically overheated *Crimes of Passion* (1984), in which she plays a fashion designer who turns into something a little sexier than a pumpkin at midnight—she becomes a hooker named China Blue. The more explicit "European" version was eventually released on these shores as an unrated home video. Here, Turner, clothed, sodomizes a cop with his own nightstick.

There's an extremely weak (but nevertheless spirited) case to be made that Turner did full-frontal nudity in the sense that she supplied the come-hither voice for Jessica Rabbit (*"I'm not really bad, I'm just drawn that way"*) in *Who Framed Roger Rabbit* (1988). It was later revealed that the full-figured cartoon character indulges in a few frames of pornographic nudity, courtesy of some sly animators and visible only on the early laserdisc edition, and then only with sophisticated frame-by-frame advance.

For a while, Turner's career seemed stalled by rumors of weight gain; she later claimed rather bizarrely that she purposely plumped up to play the mother of an autistic child in *House of Cards* (1993).

Sigourney Weaver

Undershirt in Hyperspace

Next to JACQUELINE BISSET, the woman most responsible for the film fetishization of braless undershirts is Sigourney Weaver. She wears the sheer garment to bed in hyperspace and also wears it into combat with those slimy drool-things that won't leave her alone in *Alien* and its two successors.

Weaver can also take credit for one of the best MEL GIBSON make-out scenes in movie history. In Peter Weir's underrated *The Year of Living Dangerously* (1983), Weaver and Gibson are sparring romantics until they crash a dangerous roadblock in this story of Filipino political tensions. Just as the car breaks the sentry's barricades, so do the lovers' reserves fall to pieces. They hungrily consume each other in a movie that proves the statuesque Weaver can melt a man. She later spoofed that idea good-naturedly in *Working Girl* (1988) as she tries in her undies to devour a reluctant Harrison Ford.

The stage-trained actress was born Susan Weaver on October 8, 1949, to former NBC president Sylvester Weaver and actress Elizabeth Inglis. She has

In the *Alien* series, Sigourney Weaver does for the braless undershirt look in outer space what Jackie Bisset did for it underwater.

been nominated three times for an Oscar for her work in *Aliens, Working Girl,* and *Gorillas in the Mist.*

In Roman Polanski's *Death and the Maiden* (1994), Weaver plays a woman who tries to wrangle a confession out of the man she believes raped and tortured her years before. Although at times the audience is meant to doubt her, there is a preliminary shot of Weaver's breast covered with old welts, which tips the scales of justice in her favor.

For erotic nudity in the tall, Yale-trained drama student's career you'd have to go back to 1986's *Half Moon Street,* in which Weaver plays Lauren Slaughter, a doctoral researcher by day indulging a call-girl habit by night. (A similar scenario helped KATHLEEN TURNER's career in *Crimes of Passion.*) In her call-girl persona, she has several topless scenes, including one with smitten diplomat Michael Caine, and one while riding an Exercycle—which as any woman can attest is a most uncomfortable way to work up a sweat.

But sometimes nudity itself isn't the ultimate turn-on, especially when it's in the context of a mediocre movie like *Half Moon Street.* It was that thin veneer of cotton undershirt that helped catapult Weaver's career from its shaky start in 1976's *Madman* and barely visible cameo as Woody Allen's date in 1977's *Annie Hall* to the avenging wrath of her supremely capable and confident Lt. Ellen Ripley in 1979's *Alien*.

Ripley is the only member of a futuristic spaceship crew who can effectively combat the alien that first burst rudely forth from John Hurt's stomach and then scuttles about the ship, leeching onto various humans and tunneling through their mouths to destroy them from within. Ripley is tough, fearless, wily, determined—in short, sexy. Just as in the fifties, a woman might be considered desirable if she could keep house and look good while doing it, by the late seventies, the temperature rose when Ellen Ripley could not only protect her "family"—her spaceship home, her pet cat, and the future of civilization as we know it—but had time and incentive to strip down to those BVDs for a little R&R in the cosmos. (Simultaneously, Calvin Klein's ads reworked classic cotton underwear into a symbol of erotica.)

In all three *Alien* movies, there emerged a salient image of Weaver as a feminist sex symbol—no makeup but lots of tender, maternal feelings, particularly in the first sequel when she risks personal harm to take under her wing the child survivor named Newt.

In the third and least effective installment of the series, she is finally allowed to have sex, and why not? Very few women are able to look as good as Weaver does under the conditions imposed on her in *Alien 3*—stranded on a planet full of double-Y chromosomed sex offenders, her head fully shaved due to lice.

It is a function of the screenwriter's and the director's contempt for Ripley in the third *Alien* that they kill off her beloved Newt and tender new lover (Charles Dance) and shave her head for no apparent reason. (Is it really integral to the plot that there be lice on this planet?) But Ripley's undershirt by now is truly a sign of her armor. *Alien 3* sends the series down in flames, but Ripley resides safely in the collective pop consciousness as an enduring figure of undershirted desire.

FILMOGRAPHY

Madman, 1976
Annie Hall, 1977
Alien, 1979
Eyewitness, 1980
The Year of Living Dangerously, 1983
Deal of the Century, 1983
Ghostbusters, 1984
Une Femme ou deux, 1985
Aliens, 1986
Half Moon Street, 1986
Gorillas in the Mist, 1988
Working Girl, 1988
Ghostbusters II, 1989
Helmut Newton: Frames From the Edge, 1989
Alien 3, 1991
Dave, 1993
Death and the Maiden, 1994
Copycat, 1995

. . . .
(Over) Weaver, who seems so capable her hands could be registered as lethal weapons, leans in to donate a pair of prints.
. . . .
Photo courtesy Albert Ferreira/DMI
. . . .

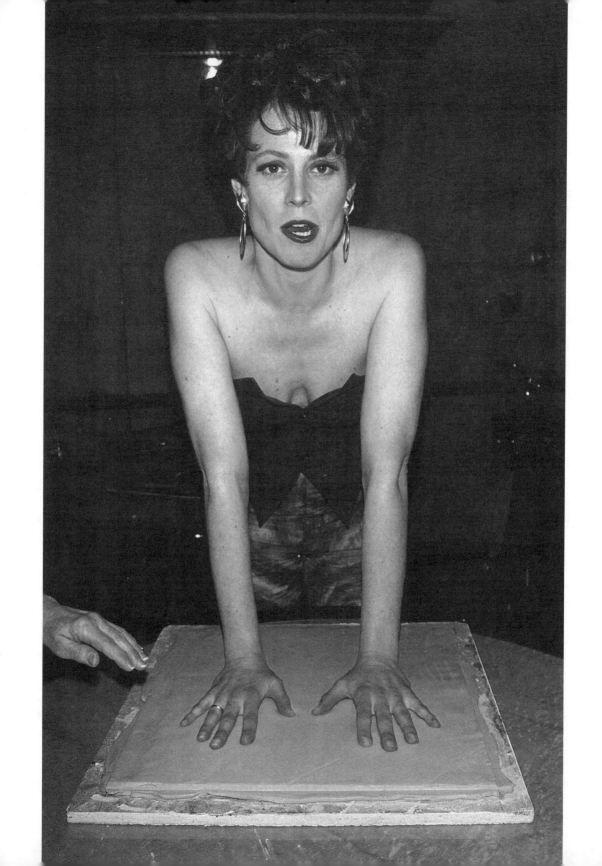

Shock Value

DON'T TELL MOM

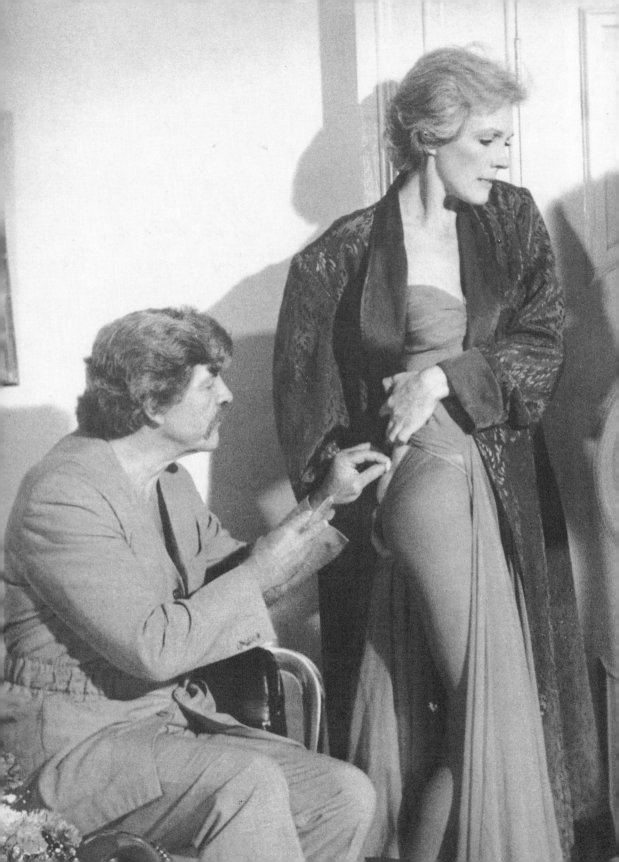

Julie Andrews

Suffering From the Sandra Dee Syndrome

You can't get much more wholesome than Julie Andrews. She was every-one's favorite nanny in *Mary Poppins* and *The Sound of Music.* She is well scrubbed. Her pronunciation is impeccable. Her clear soprano voice is like the tinkling of crystal.

So it was meant to be a bit of a shock when in *S.O.B.* (1981)—written and directed by her husband, Blake Edwards—Andrews ripped off her top and bared her breasts.

Still, it was not quite as shocking as Edwards (or even Andrews) had intended. It turns out that the actress is so squeaky clean that when she curses it's cute, when she's naked it's sweet. Try as they might, the husband-and-wife team cannot hose off the sugarcoating that still clings to Julie Andrews nearly thirty years after singing the *Do Re Mi* song.

••

Julie Andrews gets a boost in the butt from Robert Preston in S.O.B.,
the movie that pops the buttons on the former Mary Poppins.

••

F I L M O G R A P H Y

The Rose of Baghdad, 1949
Mary Poppins, 1964
The Americanization of Emily,
1964
The Sound of Music, 1965
Hawaii, 1966
Torn Curtain, 1966
Thoroughly Modern Millie, 1967
Star! 1968
Darling Lili, 1970
The Tamarind Seed, 1974
10, 1979
Little Miss Marker, 1980
S.O.B., 1981
Victor/Victoria, 1982
The Man Who Loved Women, 1983
Duet for One, 1986
That's Life!, 1986
A Fine Romance, 1992

. . . .
(Opposite) You don't need a
director yelling "Action!" to
direct the viewer's eyes as far
down as you want; the right
clothes serve the same
purpose.
. . . .
*Photo courtesy of Albert
Ferreira/DMI*
. . . .

S.O.B. is a satire of the movie business, a project into which Edwards poured his lingering resentments toward Hollywood. In it, a producer, who needs to jump-start his latest picture, trades on his actress-wife's spotless reputation by having her disrobe. The movie within a movie mirrors the real-life situation on the set of *S.O.B.*, which is kind of distasteful when you think about it.

Edwards said in interviews at the time that he wanted to prove his wife was more human than audiences imagined. When she takes off her top in the movie, it is meant as a triumphant, show-stopping moment.

Consider *Victor/Victoria* (1982), another Edwards film starring his virginal wife. Here she plays an entertainer so down and out in Paris that she reinvents herself as a man, becoming a nightclub sensation. James Garner finds himself in love and hides in the bathroom to wait for the moment of truth, which occurs off-camera. We know that he knows she's a she because his eyes widen and a smile of satisfaction and relief creeps in—satisfaction at his beloved's presumably womanly figure, and relief that he is therefore not gay for having been attracted to him/her. *Victor/Victoria* is a comedy, but if you're looking for a feeling of dangerous nightclub decadence, you'd do much better with *Cabaret*.

The British-born Andrews came into the world on October 1, 1935, as Julia Elizabeth Wells. Her talent was apparent early on, and as a child, she toured in musicals with her mother and stepfather. Although it was highly controversial to cast Audrey Hepburn as Eliza Doolittle for the film version of *My Fair Lady* when Andrews had originated the role on Broadway, the controversy boosted Andrews into the winner's seat opposite her rival on Oscar night 1964 for *Mary Poppins*.

Unfortunately, the Julie Andrews corpus does not seem capable of conjuring dirty thoughts. Instead, it reminds people how lovely it would be to have her as a nanny, as lovely asraindrops on roses and whiskers on kittens.

Drew Barrymore
From Good Genes to No Jeans

D rew Barrymore was to the Hollywood manner born. The daughter of minor B-player John Barrymore Jr., Drew's lineage is nevertheless illustrious. Her grandfather, John, was one of the greatest Hamlets of the twentieth century, a matinée idol of the silents, a legendary rake and drunk in the thirties and forties, and had the most remarked-upon profile in cinema. Her great-uncle, Lionel, made his debut as an infant in his parents' stage act and reigned as an MGM star for more than twenty years until his death. Her great-aunt, Ethel, "The First Lady of the American Stage," won an Oscar for *None but the Lonely Heart* (1944). All the Barrymores had a fondness for the demon rum.

Now Drew at a still-tender age has amassed some epithets of her own— such as being the tastiest on-screen morsel this side of E.T.'s galaxy.

Like Lionel, Drew made her debut early. At five, she played scientist WILLIAM HURT's daughter in *Altered States* (1980). Like John, she grew up to have a pretty good profile. This profile was amply displayed in the 1992 pictures *Guncrazy* and *Poison Ivy*, made when she was seventeen, and more fully revealed in all its mildly baby-fatted entirety on the covers of *Interview* and *Playboy*.

What makes it shocking that Drew turned out to be such a little sexpot is not that she traded on her noble genes to doff her jeans, but that she is best known and beloved as the little girl in *E.T.: The Extra-Terrestrial*. At age seven, she was no bigger than an extra-terrestrial herself when she played Gertie, the child who helped hide the visitor

Drew Barrymore proves too much of a temptation to her best friend's father Tom Skerritt in *Poison Ivy*, establishing Barrymore's transition to sexpot roles.

from outer space among the stuffed toys in her closet. It was so cute at that dinner table scene when this adorable child who must have memorized her lines by rote called her older brother "penis breath."

Out of the mouths of babes. Suddenly, Drew was a babe herself, exuding pheromones in such abundance that she proved irresistible to her best friend's father in *Poison Ivy*; its opening frames consist of Drew swinging provocatively in slow-motion, the object of desire in fetishistic cowboy boots. She also had the best body at the body-and-fender garage of Joey Buttafuoco in *The Amy Fisher Story*, a 1993 made-for-television movie about the famous Long Island case of the married man and the smitten minor who shot his wife in the head. On the cover of the January 1995 *Playboy*, looking mighty platinum, she wore only her butterfly, rose, and crosslet tattoos.

Most of Barrymore's screen nudity has been confined to

· ·
Barrymore sets the tone in the
opening credits of *Poison Ivy* by
swinging with a rope tight
between her bare legs.
· ·

FILMOGRAPHY

Altered States, 1980
E.T.: The Extra-Terrestrial, 1982
Firestarter, 1984
Irreconcilable Differences, 1984
Stephen King's Cat's Eye, 1985
Far From Home, 1989
See You in the Morning, 1989
Poison Ivy, 1992
Motorama, 1992
Guncrazy, 1992
Sketch Artist, 1992
Doppelganger, 1993
No Place to Hide, 1993
Bad Girls, 1994
Boys on the Side, 1995
Mad Love, 1995

wet or clingy T-shirt scenes; if she had stayed away from drugs and alcohol the way she stays away from bras she might have had a less traumatic adolescence.

Linda Blair

A Real Head-Turner

What possessed Linda Blair to pursue a career of cheesy women's prison and exploitation flicks? Perhaps it's the devil in her.

The former child model from Westport, Connecticut, received an Academy Award nomination at the tender age of fourteen for her role as the head-swiveling, pea-soup-vomiting, masturbating-with-a-crucifix child Regan in *The Exorcist* (1973). It's been downhill since.

From being the most famous child star of the moment, Blair's star burned out quickly, although she continued to work steadily. She became even more notorious for *Born Innocent* (1974), a television movie where she is raped with a broom handle by the girls in the reformatory. The camera stays on Blair from the waist up, her hands crossed over her bare breasts. *Born Innocent* made for intense television, an unvarnished look at children behind bars. Whether it amounted to serious social commentary or perverted exploitation—the rape scene was subsequently cut—it launched Blair into typecast-

FILMOGRAPHY
T
he Way We Live Now, 1970
The Sporting Club, 1971
The Exorcist, 1973
Airport 1975, 1975
Exorcist II: The Heretic, 1977
Summer of Fear, 1978
Roller Boogie, 1979
Wild Horse Hank, 1979
Hell Night, 1981
Chained Heat, 1983
Night Patrol, 1984
Savage Streets, 1984
Rote Hitze, 1985
Savage Island, 1985
Nightforce, 1987
Grotesque, 1988
Silent Assassins, 1988
Up Your Alley, 1988
Bad Blood, 1989
Witchcraft, 1989
A Woman Obsessed, 1989
Bail Out, 1990
Moving Target, 1990
Repossessed, 1990
Zapped Again, 1990
Bedroom Eyes 2, 1990
Fatal Bond, 1993

ing hell in a string of ridiculous B movies, like 1983's *Chained Heat*.

This semiparody has Blair in a bitchy women's prison, where she has to fend off advances from underclad cellmates like Sybil Danning and a raunchy warden whose office furniture conveniently includes a Jacuzzi. Although Blair was already a grown twenty-four-year-old woman when she made this, she still resembles the little girl of *The Exorcist*, which is perhaps even more frightening. At any rate, it made audiences squeamish. Blair's career is in need of an exorcism, if it's not already too late.

Linda Blair didn't seem destined for the sexy women's-prison circuit when she burst upon the scene as the demonically possessed child in *The Exorcist*.

Blair and some of the reform school gals from *Chained Heat*, modeling the formfitting regulation long johns that make prison life so erotic.

Jamie Lee Curtis

Former Horror Virgin Gets Aerobic

While not quite as pretty as her dad, Tony Curtis, or mom, Janet Leigh, in their 1950s prime, Jamie Lee Curtis nevertheless became a star in her own right. Partly it's because of her no-nonsense earthiness. Partly it's because she has a body that makes jaws drop.

Jaws first dropped in *Trading Places* (1983) when Curtis confronts Dan Aykroyd topless. Her broad shoulders, narrow waist, and lean body accentuated the vision that would be repeated in *Grandview, U.S.A.* (1984) and *Love Letters* (1983), the latter of which featured some steamy topless scenes with costar James Keach.

In *Perfect* (1985), she plays an aerobics instructor who bounces all over the place in a leotard until even the most passive viewer feels conditioned and toned.

It was a calculated shock when Curtis suddenly showed up as a frumpy housewife in *True Lies* (1994). Audiences knew this couldn't be for real—why would director James Cameron cast a body such as hers opposite a body such as ARNOLD SCHWARZENEGGER's to play marrieds if she were going to spend the movie sleeping with her mouth open, wearing dowdy clothes, and looking less appealing than pocket lint?

It was all part of the movie's elaborate joke. After an extended brush with imagined danger, Curtis's character gets in touch with her inner sensuality when she is blackmailed into doing a striptease down to a lacy Victoria's Secret thong. As she gyrates against a hotel bedpost with a man watching her from the shadows (it turns out to be Arnold), she really gets into it in a double-jointed kind of way. Curtis has said the raunchiest parts of her dance were left on the cutting-room floor.

The scene is leavened when Curtis falls over and rebounds—a vestige of her former, clumsy self—but from then on, the movie features her as a self-sufficient babe in a low-cut, hydraulically engineered dress.

Curtis has always seemed self-sufficient on-screen, even in the slew of horror vehicles that jump-started her career. In *Halloween* (1978), *The Fog* (1980), and others, Curtis is the one female who survives the carnage—thanks to keeping both her wits and her virginity. (Girls who have sex in horror movies always get killed.)

Jamie Lee Curtis finally shows a little décolletage after having started *True Lies* as Arnold Schwarzenegger's frumpy housewife.

FILMOGRAPHY

Halloween, 1978
The Fog, 1980
Prom Night, 1980
Terror Train, 1980
Halloween II, 1981
Road Games, 1981
Love Letters, 1983
Trading Places, 1983
The Adventures of Buckaroo
Banzai, 1984
Grandview, U.S.A., 1984
Perfect, 1985
Amazing Grace and Chuck, 1987
Un Homme amoureux, 1987
Dominick and Eugene, 1988
A Fish Called Wanda, 1988
Blue Steel, 1989
Queens Logic, 1991
My Girl, 1991
Forever Young, 1992
My Girl 2, 1994
Mother's Boys, 1994
True Lies, 1994
A Fish Called Wanda 2, 1995

The one-time law student, born November 22, 1958, demonstrated her comic talents in *A Fish Called Wanda* (1988) and brought out the fetishistic aspects of being a police officer in *Blue Steel* (1989). In that movie, assembling her uniform for work is filmed as erotically as if she were stripping it off.

She was virtually wasted as supportive helpmates in the *My Girl* movies (1991 and 1994) and *Forever Young* (1992), despite the presence in the latter of MEL GIBSON, who shows up on her doorstep unexpectedly after having been frozen in the past and then thawed out in the present. In *Mother's Boys* (1994), her nudity is disturbing because she is using it to arouse her adolescent son as she gets out of the bath.

True Lies rejuvenates her as a versatile leading lady and potential action heroine. Nearly a decade after playing an aerobics instructor, Curtis still has all the right muscles; she did her own stunts in the scene where she is pulled from the top of a speeding limo and dangled from a helicopter over the sea—which for action fans may be about as sexy as you can get.

Jeff Goldblum

The Bum That Launched Five Sequels (and Counting)

It's never been all that pleasant to see Jeff Goldblum naked on screen.

It's not for any physical lack on his part. The tall, slightly gawky actor is well muscled and quite handsome in person, an obvious product of some Los Angeles health club. It's not every actor who can swing from the rafters and do push-ups on the wall the way Goldblum (or a stunt double, or as a result of special effects) did in *The Fly* (1986).

It's just that the times Goldblum has bared more than his soul have involved somewhat distasteful circumstances.

Born October 22, 1952, in Pittsburgh, Goldblum trained at New York's Neighborhood Playhouse and did theater until he got his first role, as Freak 1 in the first *Death Wish* (1974). We have Goldblum's character to thank (or blame) for Charles Bronson's many-sequeled vigilante revenge spree, for it is Freak 1 who sets things in motion. "I played a rapist killer who kills Charles

FILMOGRAPHY

Death Wish, 1974
Nashville, 1975
Next Stop, Greenwich Village, 1976
Special Delivery, 1976
Annie Hall, 1977
Between the Lines, 1977
The Sentinel, 1977
Invasion of the Body Snatchers, 1978
Remember My Name, 1978
Thank God It's Friday, 1978
Threshold, 1981
The Big Chill, 1983
The Right Stuff, 1983
The Adventures of Buckaroo Banzai, 1984
Into the Night, 1985
Silverado, 1985
Transylvania 6–5000, 1985
The Fly, 1986
Beyond Therapy, 1987
Vibes, 1988
Earth Girls Are Easy, 1989
El Mono Loco/The Mad Monkey, 1989
The Tall Guy, 1989
Mister Frost, 1990
Twisted Obsession, 1990
The Favor, the Watch, and the Very Big Fish, 1992
Deep Cover, 1992
Fathers and Sons, 1992
Shooting Elizabeth, 1992
The Player, 1992
Jurassic Park, 1993
Hideaway, 1995

Bronson's wife and rapes his daughter, and there you go!" says Goldblum. "I liked the role back then; I was hungry to act."

Goldblum drops his drawers to sodomize the daughter, a rare glimpse of the Goldblum bum. The woman he rapes is so traumatized that she is diagnosed later in the movie with "catatonia, dementia praecox, passive schizoid paranoia . . . she's *almost a goddamn vegetable!*"

It makes dramatic sense in *The Fly* that Goldblum, as the hyperactive scientist Seth Brundle, would conduct his mad scientific experiments in the nude. Otherwise, his clothes might realign themselves inside out when he finishes teleporting himself from one module in his lab to another.

The Fly is a graphic remake of the 1958 Vincent Price horror film of the same name in which Price, his head affixed to the body of an insect, utters the immortal plea *"Heeelp me!"* There is a well-known publicity photo from the David Cronenberg shocker of a naked Goldblum crouching artfully inside the teleportation device. What is a little repulsive about this image is that the experiment goes awry when an ordinary housefly gets teleported along with Brundle, creating a new species—Brundlefly. He's half-human, half-pest, and exceedingly hairy.

At first, Brundle is exhilarated by his trip through the teleporter. He has increased energy and concentration. It is not until his skin starts to fall off in clumps and he seasons his food to taste by regurgitating on it that he realizes he is mutating into a housefly.

"I never went into acting to earn my fortune, I think it's bad odds if you do that," says Goldblum. "It was always a matter of following my heart—I had to act, I wanted to act in some way, and it was my appetite and joy for that which allows me to do it. It also obliterates any kind of reasonable sense of career strategy I might have."

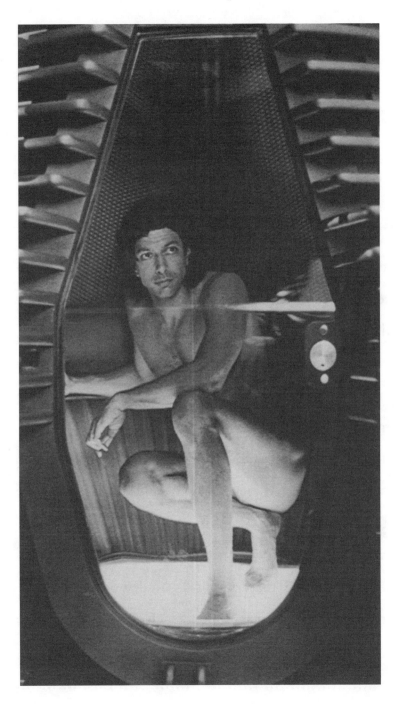

Jeff Goldblum is ready for take-off in this famous photo from *The Fly*, in which he wears nothing but his DNA for an experiment in teleportation.

Charlotte Rampling

Chimp, Chimp, Cherie

Woody Allen was once asked one of those wish-list questions, something like: Who in history would you most like to have dinner with? Among the dinner guests he requested was Charlotte Rampling.

One presumes he had ample time to have that dinner since he cast her in his semiautobiographical 1980 film *Stardust Memories* as a girlfriend with neuroses equal in measure to Allen's own.

And why wouldn't a director want to have dinner with Rampling, with her heavy-lidded sexuality, lean and graceful body, and cheekbones sharp enough to be registered weapons?

The English actress was born February 5, 1946, and has parlayed her sensuous appeal into a string of movies that occasionally borders on the bizarre.

Take, for example, Nagisa Oshima's 1986 French comedy *Max, Mon*

....

(Opposite) Charlotte Rampling gives the Nazis a sadomasochistic thrill in *Night Porter*.

....

FILMOGRAPHY

The Knack ... and How to Get It,
1965
Georgy Girl, 1966
The Long Duel, 1967
La Caduta degli dei/The Damned,
1969
How to Make It, 1969
Three, 1969
The Ski Bum, 1970
Vanishing Point, 1970
Addio, Fratello Crudele, 1971
Asylum, 1972
Corky, 1972
Giordano Bruno, 1973
Caravan to Vaccares, 1974
The Night Porter, 1974
Yuppi Du, 1974
Zardoz, 1974
Farewell, My Lovely, 1975
Foxtrot, 1975
Orca, the Killer Whale, 1977
Un Taxi mauve, 1977
Stardust Memories, 1980
The Verdict, 1982
Viva la Vie!, 1984
On ne meurt que deux fois, 1985
Tristesse et beauté, 1985
Max, mon amour, 1986
Angel Heart, 1987
Mascara, 1987
D.O.A., 1988
Paris by Night, 1988
Helmut Newton: Frames From the
Edge, 1989
Rebus, 1989

Amour, in which Rampling is unfaithful to her diplomat husband with a chimpanzee. The actress plays it completely straight, lying naked under the sheets with the simian, bending to his touch, getting hot at the dinner table with guests present when Max makes goo-goo monkey eyes at her. When the chimp lovingly strokes her hair, it is really too much.

But monkey business pales in comparison to the antics of *The Night Porter* (1974), Liliana Cavani's thoroughly twisted tale of fetishistic Nazi love, involving walking barefoot over broken glass and other sexual weirdness.

In that movie, Rampling is a former concentration camp victim who continues her affair after the war with the sadistic Nazi (Dirk Bogarde) who formerly abused her behind barbed wire. This ode to sadomasochism did not hit a very responsive chord with general audiences, but it did attract a select clientele of Rampling fans who enjoyed seeing her sing and dance in Nazi gear and suspenders, sans shirt.

Isabella Rossellini

Garter-Variety Sex

Fans more accustomed to staring at the luminous Isabella Rossellini's face in those Lancôme ads were suddenly staring at a lot more of her in *Blue Velvet*, a stunningly sick film made by Rossellini's then-boyfriend, David Lynch.

Rossellini's acting career hadn't amounted to much at the time. But perhaps, because of Lynch's personal stake in the relationship, he could easily envision her in fetishistic garters and underthings, forced into compromising sexual situations.

The controversial 1986 film unearthed the grubs in the dirt from which white picket fences rise. Lynch has always had a thing about small-town secrets—hence his cult television show *Twin Peaks*—and here he sends clean-cut Kyle MacLachlan on a nightmarish mission to find the owner of a discarded severed ear. What MacLachlan stumbles upon instead is Rossellini, a chanteuse up to both her ears in trouble.

It took then-boyfriend David Lynch to see beyond the fresh-faced exterior of the Lâncome beauty to her possibilities as the victim of sexual blackmail.

Photo courtesy of David Allocca/DMI

As Dorothy Vallens, the thirty-four-year-old Rossellini was forced to endure weird, sadistic sex with the evil Frank Booth (Dennis Hopper), a man who snorts from an inhalant while abusing her. He is holding Dorothy's husband and son hostage in return for these vile favors, which MacLachlan first witnesses voyeuristically from the closet in Dorothy's apartment where he is hiding.

"When I came out of the bushes totally naked, I felt like a slab of beef hanging," says Rossellini. "It would have felt like a sin if I was doing a nude scene to titillate the public."

Although many actresses could have played Dorothy, or looked better in those unflattering garters, Rossellini can't help bringing to everything she does an echo of her famous mother, Ingrid Bergman, a cinematic symbol of old-time romance, class, poise, and noble partings on the tarmac of the Casablanca airport. Even the scandal to which Bergman was party—leaving her husband for director Roberto Rossellini and being pregnant before her next union was legal, which cost her seven years of Hollywood acceptance—is nevertheless a scandal of the heart, one that would be perfectly acceptable by today's standards.

Seeing the saintly Ingrid Bergman's look-alike daughter under the circumstances of *Blue Velvet* took its toll. While critics raved about Lynch's breakthrough genius, many movie-goers writhed in discomfort.

Since then, Rossellini has been dressed like a man for MADONNA's *Sex* book, revealed her breasts as the cult priestess with the key to eternal life in *Death Becomes Her* (1992), and made pianoforte love with Gary Oldman's Beethoven in *Immortal Beloved* (1994). Beethoven may not have had such keen hearing, but his other senses were aquiver; Oldman and Rossellini nearly tied the knot right after making the movie.

FILMOGRAPHY

A Matter of Time, 1976
Il Prato, 1979
Il Pap'occhio, 1981
White Nights, 1985
Blue Velvet, 1986
Red Riding Hood, 1987
Siesta, 1987
Tough Guys Don't Dance, 1987
Zelly and Me, 1988
Cousins, 1989
Dames galantes, 1990
Wild at Heart, 1990
Death Becomes Her, 1992
Fearless, 1993
Wyatt Earp, 1994
Immortal Beloved, 1994

• •

Isabella Rossellini gives small-town boy Kyle MacLachlan something with which to broaden his horizons in *Blue Velvet,* **in which she engages unwillingly in weirdo sex with Dennis Hopper.**

• •

Mickey Rourke

Bare Butt, Cauliflower Ear

The question is not whether we really want to see Mickey Rourke naked, it's whether we even want to see him at all.

The once promising Rourke has been looking worse and worse in recent years, unshaven, unwashed, some teeth knocked out from the boxing bouts he insists on staging. He is one of those people who is famous for being famous, photographed at nightclubs or written up in gossip columns. His escapades include ongoing marital strife with model Carré Otis and a long-standing grudge against gossip columnist Richard Johnson, who uses ink on slow news days to challenge the pugnacious actor to a boxing match that has never materialized. (Rourke has implied that mobster John Gotti convinced him to lay off Johnson.)

Luckily, most of the nudity in Rourke's movies comes from his leading ladies. Why they would disrobe for him is anyone's guess, but it probably has to do with casting decisions beyond their control.

Born in Schenectady in 1950 and raised in Liberty City, a low-rent Miami neighborhood, Rourke is an Actors Studio graduate who, like fellow alumnus Marlon Brando, has an aversion to clear enunciation. He had a promising beginning as the arsonist of *Body Heat* (1981) and the loser hairdresser of *Diner* (1982), and has occasionally made a strong impression in such films as *The Pope of Greenwich Village* (1984) and *Barfly* (1987) as the extremely seedy poet boozer.

At the same time, Rourke has had a parallel career as a protagonist in the cinema of sexual perversion. In *9½ Weeks* (1986), he seems at first like a good catch for lonely art gallery manager KIM BASINGER. He's attentive, unpredictable, and he likes sex—lots of sex, in lots of different ways. As their relationship progresses, it's clear that Rourke's character is a sadistic nutjob who terrorizes, compromises, and humiliates his girlfriend while she begs for more. Even then, there was something about Rourke's performance that was so realistic that the movie really worked on its own terms; that is, the sexual masochists among the moviegoing public recognized the real thing when they saw it.

Rourke's butt became the butt of jokes after *Angel Heart* (1987), in which you see it writhe around with equally nude *Cosby Show* daughter Lisa Bonet while sacrificial chicken

Homeboy boxer Mickey Rourke looks about as appealing with blood streaming as he did in the naked bloodbath of *Angel Heart*, where shots of his flaccid butt got canned in order to facilitate a milder rating.

V-necked Rourke and soon-to-be-wife Carré Otis take a rare breather from what they said was genuine heavy breathing in *Wild Orchid*.

blood pours all over them. It got the movie an X rating until some of the blood was mopped up. Also lost in those trims were prolonged shots of the Rourke rear rising and falling on top of Bonet.

In 1990, Rourke made *Wild Orchid*, and the fallout from that silly movie has not stopped. Rourke costarred with the luscious Otis. Later, they married, which is no surprise—what they did with each other in the movie, or at least what they *said* they did, would make them legally wed in most states.

Otis plays a buttoned-up novice lawyer who is taken under the wing of experienced banker JACQUELINE BISSET and flown to Rio during *Carnivale*. There she falls prey to the pulsing rhythms of the drums and the rhythmic pulsing of the ear-ringed Rourke, who indoctrinates her into the more aerobic aspects of anonymous sex.

Every now and then, a movie comes along where, usually for publicity purposes, it is claimed that the sex scenes are "the real thing" instead of carefully choreographed simulated groupings. Rourke got into the spirit, gleefully admitting to the press that the sex was genuine, and that what you see on-screen isn't half of what was actually filmed. (The other half eventually showed up in a *Playboy* pictorial.)

The reward for all that horizontal hula was that Otis wed Rourke and embarked upon a tempestuous union rife with charges that he beat and stalked her. She showed up one day with a mysterious gunshot wound to the shoulder. She either did or did not bar her ex from attending her modeling runway shows in 1994, depending on which gossip column you read. "I'm not afraid of anything . . . *that has a penis*," remarked Rourke to *Entertainment Weekly*. "Get my drift?"

ELLEN BARKIN, who costarred with Rourke in *Diner* and *Johnny Handsome* (1989), defends her friend as "a great actor" who is too unpredictable for current Hollywood tastes. "Fashion seems to have moved away from the DE NIROS and Pacinos, who are scary actors," says Barkin. "You never know what they're gonna do."

Meanwhile, Rourke continues to be, like Jerry Lewis, a big hit in France, a country that takes in Hollywood's discards and recycles them as geniuses.

FILMOGRAPHY

1941, 1979
Fade to Black, 1980
Heaven's Gate, 1980
Body Heat, 1981
Diner, 1982
Eureka, 1983
Rumble Fish, 1984
The Pope of Greenwich Village, 1984
Year of the Dragon, 1985
9½ Weeks, 1986
Angel Heart, 1987
Barfly, 1987
A Prayer for the Dying, 1987
Homeboy, 1988
Francesco, 1989
Johnny Handsome, 1989
Wild Orchid, 1990
Desperate Hours, 1990
Harley Davidson & the Marlboro Man, 1991
White Sands, 1992
F.T.W., 1995
Falltime, 1995
Bullet, 1995
Guilty Conscience, 1996

This is the Rourke we know from gossip columns—rude, unsavory, yet costar to the world's most beautiful women in perverted sexual scenarios. Go figure.

Photo courtesy of David Allocca/DMI

Brooke Shields

Former Guaranteed Virgin Tries to Bust Loose

New York-born Brooke Shields was born to be photographed. Before she was a year old, she had been "discovered" by Francesco Scavullo and thus began her childhood modeling career.

In 1977, at age twelve, she made her film debut in a mediocre slasher movie variously titled *Communion*, *Holy Terror*, or *Alice, Sweet Alice*. She is bumped off mercifully early in the movie.

While still twelve, she began filming Louis Malle's *Pretty Baby*, the movie with which she is still synonymous—despite the fact that she is now a grown woman, who's no longer under the thumb of stage mother Teri.

In *Pretty Baby*, Shields was a child prostitute in the red-light Storyville district of turn of the century New Orleans. Again, she is heavily photographed—here by Keith Carradine, playing a period photographer who later marries the girl. At the next remove, she is being photographed by the film's champion cinematographer, Sven Nykvist. All in all, Shields looks pretty photogenic in *Pretty Baby*.

But there's no escaping that this naked female, auctioned off more than once as a virgin to unsuspecting customers, is really just a little girl—not only the character, but the actress behind that character. As Craig Hosoda warns with characteristic bluntness in his *Bare Facts Video Guide*, "She was eleven to twelve years old at this time so there isn't a whole lot to see here."

The subject matter and frank nudity, combined with the actress's age (and the accepted wisdom that her mom had engineered the role) led to pockets of public outcry, although one of the film's achievements is how tastefully it is handled. SUSAN SARANDON, who was assigned to watch over Shields while making the movie, saw to it that any nudity was only from the waist up. And Shields herself later paid tribute to her *Pretty Baby* director in a thesis on him called "The Voyage From Innocence to Experience."

Shields has appeared partly naked in other films, but generally it has been the work of stunt doubles. In such adolescent erotica as *Endless Love* (1981) and *The Blue Lagoon* (1980), Shields still comes out seeming as wholesome as when she posed as the baby on the Ivory Snow box.

How ironic that the Princeton grad would later be associated not with sex, but with celibacy. She lent her name to a huge publicity campaign for a book she wrote, *On Your Own*, about the virtuous teenage life. Allegedly, her contract stipu-

In *Pretty Baby* Brooke Shields is a professional child virgin in the house of ill repute where her mom Susan Sarandon works.

People still think of her as a kid, but Shields, while preparing for her Broadway role in *Grease*, has the washboard abs of a full-grown woman.

FILMOGRAPHY

Alice, Sweet Alice, 1977
King of the Gypsies, 1978
Pretty Baby, 1978
Just You and Me, Kid, 1979
Tilt, 1979
Wanda Nevada, 1979
The Blue Lagoon, 1980
Endless Love, 1981
The Muppets Take Manhattan, 1984
Sahara, 1984
Brenda Starr, 1989 (released 1992)
Speed Zone, 1989
Backstreet Dreams, 1990
Legends in Light (documentary), 1993
Freaked, 1993

lated that she guaranteed she was still a virgin (and hopefully would remain so at least until she finished stumping for the book). When she announced in late 1994 that she was stepping into the role of bad-girl Rizzo in the Broadway revival of *Grease*, audiences were alarmed.

"People have trouble seeing me as an adult," Shields complained after her first mature role in *Backstreet Dreams*. "They remember me as a teenager, and they have trouble making the transition. I mean, I'm a grown woman!"

Full-Frontal Assault

THE FINAL FRONTIER

Ellen Barkin

A Change of Luck

Before she married (and divorced) Gabriel Byrne and had two babies, Ellen Barkin lived in a SoHo loft, choosing her film projects with care and spending much of her free time at the gym. It was no secret that her off-kilter beauty was complemented by a well balanced Nautilus body.

You can see every inch of that well defined body in *Siesta*, a 1987 arthouse film that flopped despite a cast that included JODIE FOSTER in one of her first post-Yale appearances, Martin Sheen, ISABELLA ROSSELLINI, and Byrne—who met his future (and future ex-) wife on the set. Perhaps it helped that the role required her to suck his finger.

Previously, Barkin's sexuality was highlighted by the famous bedroom scene in *The Big Easy* (1987), in which Dennis Quaid is a self-assured New

Barkin on the set of *Man Trouble*; allure enough for two, but unfortunately, not enough to revive this comedy costarring Jack Nicholson as a dog trainer.

Ellen Barkin lets her body do the talking to Al Pacino in *Sea of Love,* although some of her nude scenes were courtesy of a body double.

Orleans cop who puts his hand up her skirt and promises, "Darlin', your luck is about to change." It does, too.

As effective as that scene was, Barkin kept all her clothes on. "Sometimes sex scenes are good because they're sex scenes, because they're sexy, and good directors direct them and they know how to direct them. But that's rare," says Barkin. "I think probably what makes a good sex scene is that maybe you find something out about the character in the course of the scene, instead of just seeing them have some sex act transpire before your eyes."

In *Siesta,* an experimental film, Barkin plays an obsessional tightrope walker who may or may not be party to a murder. She has several full-frontal nude scenes, but there's no need to call the morals squad—this is an art film. You can tell it's an art film because it is largely incomprehensible. In fact, if it weren't for Barkin's nudity there would be little reason to watch it all the way through, unless you want to hear Foster do an upper-crust British accent.

In *Sea of Love,* two years later, Barkin has some hot scenes with cop Al Pacino, but part of the heat is generated by not knowing whether Barkin is in fact the killer Pacino is seeking. A body double stood in for Barkin's left breast in the initial seduction scene.

"I think what makes a great movie actor is just someone up there telling you the truth about whatever they're feeling at that moment. They're telling you a secret about themselves," says Barkin. "With Marlon Brando, you were always looking at something that you didn't think you should be privy to. You didn't think you should be allowed to know someone so intimately."

Barkin's steamy, amoral sex scenes with fellow conman Laurence Fishburne in *Bad Company* (1995) were remarkable in that the two were Hollywood's first interracial couple for whom race was not an issue.

Barkin is known for voicing her strong opinions, *strongly.* One of her pet peeves is how her profession, with its emphasis on sex scenes, is riddled with people chosen for looks alone. "No one would think of going up to a firm, attractive young girl with small breasts and saying, here's a pair of toeshoes, you look right, maybe you could be a ballet dancer and dance *Swan Lake.* But with acting, people seem to think that anybody could do that if you look appropriate for the role."

FILMOGRAPHY

Diner, 1982
Tender Mercies, 1983
Daniel, 1983
Eddie and the Cruisers, 1983
Enormous Changes at the Last Minute, 1983
The Adventures of Buckaroo Banzai, 1984
Harry and Son, 1984
Terminal Choice, 1985
Desert Bloom, 1986
Down by Law, 1986
The Big Easy, 1987
Made in Heaven, 1987
Siesta, 1987
Johnny Handsome, 1989
Sea of Love, 1989
Switch, 1991
Man Trouble, 1992
This Boy's Life, 1993
Into the West, 1993
Bad Company, 1995

Willem Dafoe

"Love Scenes Are Pure Action."

Y̆ou have only to catch some of Willem Dafoe's performances at the Wooster Group experimental theater in SoHo, of which he has been a member for years, to know that Dafoe has no hang-ups about performing in the nude. In one such theater piece, he danced crazily around the stage in a grass hula skirt, wearing nothing underneath.

Small and wiry, frequently as intense in person as he appears on-screen, the Wisconsin-born Dafoe takes many risks in his choice of roles. You can't get more controversial than playing a naked, anxiety-ridden Jesus on the cross (in *Last Temptation of Christ*, 1988) or a skeletal death-camp boxer (in *Triumph of the Spirit*, 1989).

"I think I can be a light, fluffy person, too," he complains. "I think there's a perception from the work I've done already that there's something dramatic or heavy or authoritative about my performing. I don't want a kind of film persona to harden on me and stare me back in the face and take all the joy and fun out of what I do. I want different things to remain available to me in the process of a career, always trying to jumble expectations somewhat so people can be more broadminded in how they see me. In a lot of my roles, I work through something of a mask. There's been a strong physical stamp, a strong condition. Sometimes, that's great, it makes you jump off normal behavior and do something a little extraordinary. But I'm really interested in doing something where I look more like myself, where I act more like myself, where there's a little more female energy around."

As gifted as Dafoe is physically—his anatomy was a cheery conversation stopper among theatergoers for years before he became a movie star—he is such a good actor that under certain conditions, the thought of sex with him can drive a girl to wince. That's what happens in *Wild at Heart* (1990), where he is a rotten-toothed psychopath who pinches LAURA DERN's face as foreplay.

Then in *Body of Evidence* (1993), he plays a lawyer who is such a sap you have to feel sorry for him succumbing to client MADONNA's sexual preferences, which include grinding his back onto a car hood full of glass shards and handcuffing him uncomfortably while she drips hot wax on his chest.

"I like action scenes, and love scenes are pure action for the most part," says Dafoe, born July 22, 1955.

Body of Evidence was a complete failure at the box office,

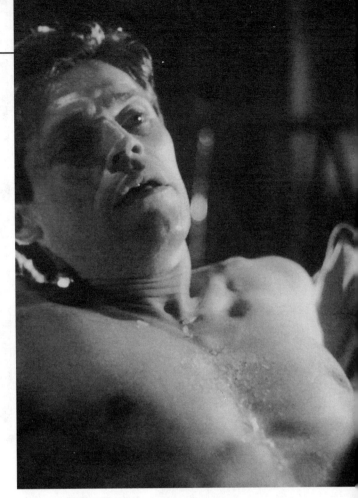

Willem Dafoe gets a hot wax job from Madonna in *Body of Evidence*, one of the less painful things she does to him in bed.

Dafoe in an uncharacteristically calculated beefcake pose.

FILMOGRAPHY

Heaven's Gate (cameo), 1980
The Loveless, 1981
New York Nights, 1982
The Hunger, 1983
The Communists Are Comfortable
(and Three Other Stories), 1984
Roadhouse 66, 1984
Streets of Fire, 1984
To Live and Die in L.A., 1985
Platoon, 1986
Dear America, 1987
The Last Temptation of Christ,
1988
Mississippi Burning, 1988
Off Limits, 1988
Born on the Fourth of July, 1989
Triumph of the Spirit, 1989
Cry-Baby, 1990
Wild at Heart, 1990
Flight of the Intruder, 1991
The Doors, 1991
Light Sleeper, 1992
White Sands, 1992
Blast 'Em (documentary), 1992
Body of Evidence, 1993
Faraway, So Close, 1993
Clear and Present Danger, 1994
Tom & Viv, 1994

but Dafoe figured after the backlash against Martin Scorsese over *Last Temptation* that the public had laid the blame on the director's doorstep, not on his. "I think they cut actors slack and say, ah, they're a bunch of whores, they've gotta make a living," he says.

Body of Evidence tried but failed to get mileage out of its casting coup. Madonna plays a sex machine who is so good in bed she gives her lovers fatal heart attacks. It is unclear whether the brief glimpses of Dafoe's family jewels are purposely designed to raise the temperature or whether they resulted from poor "blocking" of the action. Sex scenes are notorious for their complicated choreography so that nothing X-rated ever hits the camera; some of Dafoe's scenery may have been inadvertent as the actors grappled with each other in take after take.

For all its hype as a sexy film noir featuring kinky tastes and forbidden playthings, *Body of Evidence* got lousy reviews and tepid response. Sex on a bed of broken glass may be a turn-on for a select group, but mass audiences don't want to mix their pleasure with all those crunching sounds.

Jaye Davidson

Knowing All There Is to Know About the Crying Game

If you haven't yet seen *The Crying Game* (1992), well, nuts to you. The long-touted "secret" is about as secret by now as who's buried in Grant's Tomb.

Actually, the secret is a bit of a red herring, since the gender of Jaye Davidson's character is not really the key to Neil Jordan's movie. The "secret" was mostly a clever marketing gimmick by Miramax to promote a small British film that might have proved too esoteric to attract a substantial American audience. It is about love, loyalty, and being true to one's nature, but it is not an easily pigeonholed romance. Boy meets girl, boy finds out girl's a boy (and throws up), boy sticks by boy just as he promised—not necessarily because he's gay, but because it is his nature, according to the movie's twice-told metaphor about how you can neither trust a scorpion, nor can you blame it when it stings.

A soft-hearted Irish Republican Army volunteer (Stephen Rea), guilty

Stephen Rea doesn't yet know the "secret" as he kisses hair-dresser Jaye Davidson in *The Crying Game*.

Photo courtesy of Photofest

over the death of the British soldier he was guarding (Forest Whitaker), goes to London to look up the dead man's alluring hairdresser-lover and take care of her as he promised. This hairdresser, Dil (Davidson), is a piece of work even before the gender issue arises. Graceful and throaty, she gets up at the local bar to sing a mesmerizing version of "The Crying Game." Those who guessed the "secret" guessed it right there from the size of Davidson's man-sized wrists.

During the pivotal scene, Dil returns to the bed after undressing completely in the bathroom. The camera moves slowly down Dil's body, and although the chest is a giveaway, it takes both Rea's character and the audience those extra few seconds to adjust to what they're seeing, culminating in a very unambiguous shot of Davidson's privates (wrapped in a clear condom, although the shock has prevented viewers from noticing this).

The scene is indeed shocking. But what some viewers may not realize at first is that the shock is not so much the gender confusion or seeing a penis in closeup, but that this sudden information refigures all that has gone before. The mind reels back over every detail of the movie to look for clues, to reassess impressions. In fact, *The Crying Game* is more rewarding on second viewing because Jordan's Oscar-winning screenplay has cleverly foreshadowed everything.

The androgynous, delicately featured Davidson was born in Riverside, California, to an African father and British mother. He moved with his family to Hertfordshire, England, as a toddler in 1968. He studied ballet as a child, and although he quickly tired of its demands, a vestige of those studies survives in the grace with which he carries himself.

His "discovery" is the equivalent of the Lana Turner-at-Schwab's story, only this one is true. He was spotted at the wrap party for Derek Jarman's *Edward II* and cast in *The Crying Game* with no previous acting experience. (Among the jobs he has held, he really was a hairdresser at one time.)

Davidson had special costumes designed to disguise his brand-new nipple rings in *StarGate*, playing the sun god Ra surrounded by a retinue of young slave boys.

The speculation was whether the Supporting Actor nominee would attend the Oscars in drag (he chose something androgynous). There were jokes about whether he belonged in the Supporting Actor or Actress category, and whether this alone was enough to reveal the "secret" everyone was still trying to keep.

Davidson didn't win the Oscar, but began showing up in the New York gossip columns as a diva who hated to go unrecognized at trendy nightclubs. He told *Interview* magazine that after he tore through his *Crying Game* paycheck he was so broke his phone service was cut off.

FILMOGRAPHY

The Crying Game, 1992
StarGate, 1994

When the *StarGate* folks sent around a courier with his second movie offer, he had to call them back from a pay phone. "I thought, 'No, I don't think I really want to do it.' So, I said, 'All right, I'll do it for a million dollars.' I thought I had no chance of getting a million dollars. They said I had to phone back in an hour. And then when I called back, they said, 'Yeah, we'll give you a million dollars.'"

In *StarGate*, he's the sun god Ra in a stilted performance that does not show him to best advantage. It doesn't even show his nipple rings to best advantage—the costume designer thought that nipple rings might not be appropriate for a sun god, so when Davidson refused to remove them (it was a new piercing, and he didn't want to risk infection), a costume had to be fashioned loosely around them. Davidson was the only one in the cast who could not manage the special hieroglyph language convincingly, so his voice was electronically enhanced to disguise the problem. The role was effective only if you think it stylish that a sun god have an entourage of semiclad children.

Davidson's *Crying Game* nudity had at least one unintended effect—the departure of Billy Crystal as emcee of the Oscars. Crystal clashed with the telecast's producers when they wouldn't allow him to open the show with a song and dance number in which he planned to wear a skirt, under which would dangle a small golden statuette.

The producers' objections were certainly not because they were worried about spoiling the "surprise." Crystal was forced to scrap the number at the last minute and settle for previous Supporting Actor winner Jack Palance pulling an enormous Oscar onto the stage from a rope clenched in his teeth. The normally unruffled Crystal seemed kvetchy that night, and he stepped down the following year.

Robert De Niro

Frankenstein's Monster in a Birthday Suit

"Maybe I should do more sit-ups," says Robert De Niro shyly and rather hilariously when he first takes his clothes off for UMA THURMAN in *Mad Dog and Glory* (1993).

Luckily, we don't get to see him naked in that movie. By this point in his career, the thought of De Niro naked is not likely to turn anyone on. He specializes in playing psychos, madmen, obsessives, and killers, and because he plays them so well and so intensely, it's hard to imagine him in a romantic interlude.

It was all different back in 1976, when the New York-born Method actor made Bertolucci's *1900* with GERARD DEPARDIEU. Only when certain scenes were restored in 1992 were audiences able to see the two actors share a bed with an epileptic prostitute. The ceiling-mounted camera gazes down at the tableau, which includes De Niro and Depardieu lying on their backs completely in the buff, casually stroking themselves. De Niro exhibits some of the

shy, self-conscious quality that he brings to his infrequent lighter roles; as a Method actor who prizes reality above all, maybe he was in fact nervous.

Both men were young and slender at the time (De Niro was thirty-three). Depardieu is still going *à poil*, proving that in France, being a spring chicken is no prerequisite for full-frontal nudity. And now, after nearly two decades with rarely a shirt off, De Niro is once again naked on film, or at least as naked as latex allows. It doesn't matter how many sit-ups he's done, it's still not a pretty sight.

In *Mary Shelley's Frankenstein* (1994), De Niro plays the monster, and he seems as if he's in his birthday suit for the scene

in which he is "born," created by Dr. Frankenstein (Kenneth Branagh) out of stitched-together corpses and an electrical shock. De Niro comes out of his birthing tank in a sea of slippery amniotic fluid, stuffed into latex with a flopping latex penis and looking like a beat-up Michelin man. He and Branagh grapple and slide around until the monster gets his sea legs.

"We're rolling around in this fluid, which is actually warmed K–Y Jelly," said Branagh of the scene. "He's total dead weight and the prosthetic suit is splitting at the stitches, and he's totally naked underneath. I must say, it was a very intimate way of getting to know an international acting legend."

FILMOGRAPHY

Greetings, 1968
The Wedding Party, 1969
Bloody Mama, 1970
Hi, Mom!, 1970
Born to Win, 1971
The Gang That Couldn't Shoot Straight, 1971
Jennifer on My Mind, 1971
Sam's Song, 1971
Bang the Drum Slowly, 1973
Mean Streets, 1973
The Godfather, Part II, 1974
1900, 1976
The Last Tycoon, 1976
Taxi Driver, 1976
New York, New York, 1977
The Deer Hunter, 1978
Raging Bull, 1980
True Confessions, 1981
The King of Comedy, 1983
Falling in Love, 1984
Once Upon a Time in America, 1984
Brazil, 1985
The Mission, 1986
Angel Heart, 1987
The Untouchables, 1987
Midnight Run, 1988
Jacknife, 1989
We're No Angels,1989
Awakenings, 1990
Goodfellas, 1990
Stanley & Iris, 1990
Backdraft, 1991
Cape Fear, 1991
Guilty by Suspicion, 1991
Mistress, 1992
Night and the City, 1992
A Bronx Tale, 1993
Mad Dog and Glory, 1993
This Boy's Life, 1993
Mary Shelley's Frankenstein, 1994
Casino, 1995

Saxaphonist De Niro and singer Liza Minnelli as on-again off-again husband and wife during the Big Band era in *New York, New York*. Whatever he's got, it's not good enough—she leaves him by movie's end.

Richard Gere

X-Rated Thought Waves

R ichard Gere stood there as a presenter at the 1993 Oscars in front of an audience of a billion, sending his thought waves overseas in hopes of alleviating the suffering of Tibetan monks persecuted by the conquering Chinese. While he urged everyone to help him concentrate on China, most viewers were probably concentrating—as they are apt to do when in range of the now silver-haired actor—on Gere's sheer physical beauty. It may not help the Tibetan monks, but it gets a lot of folks through the night.

Gere, born August 31, 1949, was one of the first American stars to do full-frontal nudity on-screen, in 1980's *American Gigolo* (and then again in 1983's *Breathless*). He was a great dresser (and undresser) in *American Gigolo*, a smooth L.A. ladykiller-for-hire who dresses impeccably in Armani suits and keeps in shape by hanging upside down clad mostly in those trendy early eighties gravitational boots. This latter detail was a natural for the former farmboy from Syracuse because he originally arrived at the University of

Gere and various body parts
defy gravity in *American Gigolo*,
becoming one of the first
known American male stars to
display full-frontal nudity.

Massachusetts on a gymnastics scholarship.

Which also explains that little workout scene in 1977's *Looking for Mr. Goodbar*, where he falls to the floor of DIANE KEATON's bedroom and does push-ups in a jockstrap and leather jacket. In that movie, Keaton's frenetic social life eventually kills her when she meets a psychotic closet case.

Gere has been semifabulous in one fabulous movie (as a migrant worker in Terence Malick's *Days of Heaven*, 1978) and really fabulous in one shocking career resurrection (as an ultratough cop in *Internal Affairs*, 1990). But every time he hits the jackpot, it has been in thump-go-the-heartstrings movies. He's an old-fashioned romantic idol with a postwar hipness, a man willing to parade his body unselfconsciously yet sneer when it gives viewers a thrill—as it did in *Breathless* (1983), which featured brief full-frontal nudity with Valerie Kaprisky.

Gere does "self-involved" better than most, and maybe it's not all an act. Debra Winger said the two of them were oil and water on the set of the Cinderella story *An Officer and a Gentleman* (1982), which must have made it hell to film those hot love scenes. And the plot of the hugely successful *Pretty Woman* (1990) is pretty vile if you examine it closely—Gere is a cold businessman so unable to relate to women that he buys a hooker (JULIA ROBERTS) for a weekend, and after he remakes her Pygmalion-style, they fall in love.

"I hate talking about myself," says Gere about why he

ducks interviewers who harp on his erotic appeal. "I don't recognize that. I'm not really aware of those things." *Oh.*

One thing Gere may want to do in the future, aside from
sending brainwaves E-mail to the Far East, is to avoid roles
where he is on either end of the analyst's couch. In *Final
Analysis*, he is a shrink who steamily beds his patient's sister
(KIM BASINGER), thus violating a host of ethical considerations
in order for the movie to showcase his butt. And in *Mr. Jones*,
he is a manic-depressive who entices the doctor, LENA OLIN, to
join him on the couch for a little one-on-one therapy. Neither
movie was very convincing. Gere is pretty, but he's a show-
boat; look, but don't touch.

**Richard Gere hoses down with
the other soldiers in *Yanks*.**

FILMOGRAPHY

Report to the Commissioner, 1975
Baby Blue Marine, 1975
Looking for Mr. Goodbar, 1977
Bloodbrothers, 1978
Days of Heaven, 1978
Yanks, 1979
American Gigolo, 1980
An Officer and a Gentleman, 1982
Beyond the Limit, 1983
Breathless, 1983
The Cotton Club, 1984
King David, 1985
No Mercy, 1986
Power, 1986
Miles From Home, 1988
Internal Affairs, 1990
Pretty Woman, 1990
Rhapsody in August, 1991
Final Analysis (also executive producer), 1992
Mr. Jones (also executive producer), 1993
Sommersby (also executive producer), 1993
Intersection, 1994
First Knight, 1995
Primal Fear, 1996

Gere has been dogged by rumors that he is gay, to the point where he and wife Cindy Crawford took out a $30,000 ad in a London paper to refute the allegations. In any case, at least one woman kissed and told; Dawn Steel, who would become the first woman to head a major Hollywood studio (Columbia Pictures), wrote in her autobiography, *They Can Kill You But They Can't Eat You*, that she began a wild affair with Gere in 1975 after meeting him at a poker game. Although she was concerned that he was the better-looking half of the couple, "our affair was very playful, very passionate," she reported. He was "wonderfully charming, handsome, sexual, interesting, but cut off."

Cut off to some, but connected through the mental Internet to parts unknown.

William Hurt

Shadow Puppet

When Taiwan bestowed the Golden Horse Award on William Hurt in 1989 for *The Accidental Tourist*, it was not some obscure joke regarding his privates. If it were, they would have given him their version of the Oscar for *Broadcast News*.

In that 1987 movie he plays an admittedly shallow newscaster who is all style and no substance—except in bed, which is where he tries all movie long to land overachieving news producer Holly Hunter. After making love with Hunter's rival, Hurt gets out of bed, and his semierect penis makes a shadow puppet on the wall. His lover duly and appreciatively notices him, and so can the viewer equipped with a VCR freeze frame.

Hurt was born in Washington, D.C., on March 20, 1950, then raised in the South Pacific until his parents divorced. At ten, he moved with his mother and two brothers to the Upper West Side of Manhattan. (His mother remarried *Time* magazine heir Henry Luce III.) He studied theology at Tufts, but switched late in the game to theater, ending up at Juilliard and New York's Circle Rep.

In 1980, he climbed naked and ecstatic from the isolation tank of *Altered States* (1980)—his privates are visible only in the theatrical version, not on home video—and into a flourishing career as an introspective leading man. Hurt begins and ends his film debut in the nude, as befits a movie about a scientist searching for the pure essence of humanity, the naked truth of existence. He searches for this in isolation tanks, tanked up on ancient Mexican hallucinogens, as he attempts to regress both mind and body to a primordial state.

Meanwhile, Hurt's character's wife, Blair Brown, describes their lovemaking: "I feel like I'm being harpooned by some raging monk in the act of receiving God," sensible in light of Hurt's background in theology.

In an age of musclebound action heroes, Hurt has been the intellectual antidote, the thinking person's turn-on, an occasionally naked navel-gazer. Hurt usually plays characters with some pronounced Achilles

....
William Hurt, out of the isolation tank and into the arms of wife Blair Brown in *Altered States.*
....
Photo courtesy of Photofest
....

heel. That heel turns out to be his spine in *Body Heat* (1981) as he does whatever sultry KATHLEEN TURNER tells him to. And in *The Big Chill* (1983), Vietnam has gotten him so messed up, he's impotent.

You can't say that about his tortured personal life, which has tended to offset his preppie, princely screen reputation. His marital travails provide periodic fodder for Manhattan courtroom enthusiasts. First divorced from actress Mary Beth Hurt, he had a highly public child custody suit with live-in lover and one-time ballerina Sandra Jennings in 1989. Jennings accused Hurt of beating her when he drank, but his new girlfriend and future wife (and future ex-wife) Heidi Henderson—they met during a mutual stint in drug rehab—stuck by him through the trial. (But not for long—they divorced in 1993 after having two sons.)

Also a Hurt enthusiast, at least before their rancorous breakup, was Marlee Matlin, who made *Children of a Lesser God* with him in 1986.

The latest chapter in Hurt's busy social schedule involves France's Generation-X star Sandrine Bonnaire, who gave birth to their daughter in early 1994.

Hurt's career was at its peak in 1985 when he won an Oscar for playing the duplicitous gay window dresser behind bars in Hector Babenco's *Kiss of the Spider Woman*. After making that movie, he told *American Film* that he liked the challenge of that role because "to me it's much harder to be mediocre. My image is of a horse that wants to run, and the rider keeps pulling on the reins so hard that the horse's head gets turned in on itself. It's awful. It's a horrible thing to go through or do to an animal. It's happened to me. Because sometimes I feel like a horse. I want to run!"

Fortuitously then, there was the Golden Horse Award.

More seriously, Hurt's early fears that his thinning hair would be a liability have not proven true, although his career has turned more toward character parts—men stuck in their own psychic isolation tanks, bringing his career full circle.

FILMOGRAPHY

Altered States, 1980
Eyewitness, 1980
Body Heat, 1981
The Big Chill, 1983
Gorky Park, 1983
Kiss of the Spider Woman, 1985
Children of a Lesser God, 1986
Broadcast News, 1987
The Accidental Tourist, 1988
A Time of Destiny, 1988
Alice, 1990
I Love You to Death, 1990
Until the End of the World, 1991
The Doctor, 1991
The Plague, 1992
Mr. Wonderful, 1993
Trial by Jury, 1994
Second Best, 1994
Jane Eyre, 1995

Jeremy Irons
The Control Freak Freaks Out

Jeremy Irons may be skinny, with an unhealthy pallor and the look of someone who never stops smoking, but many women find him irresistible. He has made love on film to MERYL STREEP, Glenn Close, Genevieve Bujold, and JULIETTE BINOCHE, and still seems inexhaustible.

Irons is an actor whose icy exterior belies the raging caldron beneath. In *Damage* (1992), he and Binoche go at their illicit affair every which way, leaning against a public doorframe, on top of a cluttered desk, clinging to an unadorned curtain rod in a barely furnished rental flat. Irons bangs Binoche's head repeatedly against a thinly carpeted floor, and they rock so violently it merits sponsoring by the World Wrestling Federation. The point of the movie is that obsessional love is beyond anyone's comprehension, and that it is particularly devastating for control freaks like Irons's character, a repressed politician. Anyway, it is bound to end badly when your lover is betrothed to your son.

The British actor, born September 19, 1948, started his film career as a romantic lead, which has left an interesting overlay on the kind of roles he has since come to excel at—really warped characters like the morbid twin gynecologists in David Cronenberg's *Dead Ringers* (1988) and the possibly murderous faux aristocrat Claus von Bulow in Barbet Schroeder's *Reversal of Fortune* (1990), for which he won an Oscar. Playing a man who is seeing his son's girlfriend on the sly is right up his alley; the sex scenes, though not strictly erotic, provide a sick fascination.

"One tends to accept interesting roles when they are offered," said Irons cautiously from behind a pair of movie-star sunglasses. "I do love romantic stories, because you get to play with great ladies. But I do like the dark side."

Director Louis Malle managed to capture both the dark side of obsession in *Damage* and the shadowy side of nudity. It

Jeremy Irons leans in for the kiss, not realizing (even from the five o'clock shadow) that John Lone is a man in *M. Butterfly*, based on a famous true story.

Lone gets even more personal with Irons in the boudoir. One of the best moments in the film is the look of surprise, confusion, and revulsion that quickly pass over Irons's face in court when his longtime "wife" shows up dressed in suit and tie.

FILMOGRAPHY

Nijinsky, 1980
The French Lieutenant's Woman, 1981
The Masterbuilders (narrator), 1982
Moonlighting, 1982
The Wild Duck, 1982
Betrayal, 1983
Swann in Love, 1984
The Mission, 1986
Dead Ringers, 1988
Australia, 1989
A Chorus of Disapproval, 1989
Danny, the Champion of the World, 1989
Reversal of Fortune, 1990
Kafka, 1991
The Beggar's Opera, 1991
Waterland, 1992
Damage, 1992
M. Butterfly, 1993
The House of the Spirits, 1993
The Lion King (voice), 1994

is no mistake that most male nude scenes are staged in areas where something horizontal can cut the screen at that delicate juncture; otherwise the MPAA's rating board sharpens the cudgels. So, one can appreciate the artfully staged scene where the protagonist races down a winding staircase with a graceful banister doing a fair job of keeping Jeremy's irons out of the fire. In any case, the R-rated video version doesn't have as much detail as the unrated "director's cut."

Don Johnson

Nude Yoga as the Door to Sexual Enlightenment

When he played Detective Sonny Crockett on the wildly successful eighties television show Miami Vice, Don Johnson never wore socks. Back when he made The Harrad Experiment, he didn't wear anything.

The Harrad Experiment, shot in 1973 when the Missouri boy was in his early twenties and looking very coltish, was meant to be sensational at the time because it depicted a swinging alternative college where the students get a heavy dose of sex education in coed dorms and lectures. Bruno Kirby Jr. is another student who lets it all hang out during nude yoga class.

In fact, the movie is not nearly as wild as it wanted audiences to believe. Tippi Hedren plays a professor who lectures Johnson on the responsibilities of free sex—as well she should, because in real life she is the mother of MELANIE GRIFFITH, who at fourteen was an extra in the movie while visiting her mother on the set. Behind the scenes, she and Johnson were doing a little nude yoga of their own, starting what has proved to be a lifelong on-and-off

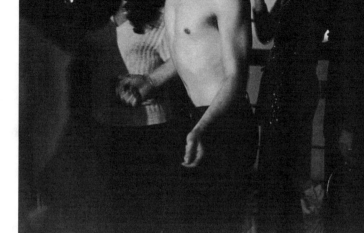

FILMOGRAPHY

The Magic Garden of Stanley
Sweetheart, 1970
Zachariah, 1970
The Harrad Experiment, 1973
A Boy and His Dog, 1974
Return to Macon County, 1975
Melanie, 1981
Cease Fire, 1985
G.I. Joe: The Movie (voice), 1987
Sweet Hearts Dance, 1988
Dead-Bang, 1989
The Hot Spot, 1990
Harley Davidson & the Marlboro
Man, 1991
Paradise, 1991
Born Yesterday, 1993
Guilty as Sin, 1993

relationship. They have married and split up twice; the second time, she got the kids, and he got drug rehab.

Johnson has a sexually dangerous quality that is exciting on-screen, an affable I'll-try-anything attitude that in a woman would be considered sluttish. He's always rumpled, as if he just got out of bed and would be quite willing to get back in. And he always has a rakish smile plastered over his face (when he was younger, the smile was more on the order of goofy).

He easily lets Virginia Madsen make a studmuffin of him in *The Hot Spot* (1990), and he's sweatily insolent with Cybil Shepherd in the television miniseries *The Long Hot Summer*. In 1993's *Guilty As Sin*, he is so irresistible he seduces his lawyer (Rebecca De Mornay) even though she knows he might have thrown his wife out a window. (Johnson told writer Joe Leydon that he loved "playing someone who lived up to everyone's worst suspicions.")

Through *Miami Vice*, Johnson helped make pastels acceptable, and day-old stubble is still referred to in some circles as the Don Johnson Look. Somehow, the nude yoga never caught on.

Harvey Keitel

Nothing But Maori Stripes and a Feather Duster

Piano a little dusty? Send for Harvey Keitel.

It may take years before New Yorker Keitel, a serious actor with an impressive resumé, can live down the nude housekeeping scene from *The Piano*, in which all he wears are the Maori stripes on his forehead. That *The Piano* is a beautiful, sensitive film that won numerous Oscars does not change the fact that Keitel has been ridiculed mercilessly ever since.

The intense actor, born in 1941, has spent a career gravitating toward important directors, rather than going for the easy Hollywood buck. An alumnus of New York's Actors Studio, he was most identified with his work for Martin Scorsese, including *Mean Streets* (1973) and *Taxi Driver* (1976).

Then came the one-two punch of *Bad Lieutenant* in 1992 and *The Piano* in 1993. With those two splashy movies, Keitel became poster boy for male full-frontal nudity.

Harvey Keitel has already sacrificed several black keys to get this far with Holly Hunter in his barter system of letting her buy back her precious piano, one black key at a time, in return for sensual favors in *The Piano*.

Bad Lieutenant is Abel Ferrara's tough, apocalyptic story of a dirty New York cop's fast and furious descent into hell. He is helped along by a drug habit—he steals it, shoots it, and snorts it off a photo of his wife and kids. He takes payoffs from criminals, bets the mortgage, smokes crack with dealers, and lives his life about as far down the drain as you can get.

After an orgy of sex, drugs, and self-loathing, the lieutenant—he is so bad he doesn't even have a name—lets loose gut-wrenching sobs in a scene of full-frontal nudity that helped earn the movie its NC–17 rating, and which looks like the mirror-smashing scene he never got to play when he relinquished his role to Martin Sheen in *Apocalypse Now* (1979). Keitel had shot a considerable amount of footage on that film before he was replaced due to the usual "artistic differences."

Because *Bad Lieutenant* deals with the possibility of redemption in a worst-case-scenario world, the director, Abel Ferrara, plunges the viewer into sordid scenes that are successively harder to take. The toughest is a creepily extended one in which Keitel approaches two teenage girls loitering in their car, and forces them to enable his masturbatory fantasies in return for not reporting them to their strict suburban dad. He has one of them pull down the back of her underwear, the other one feign oral sex out the car window while he stimulates himself. His repetition of pornographic phrases is like a religious mantra.

At its premiere at the Toronto International Film Festival, *Bad Lieutenant* drew seesawing reactions, ranging from euphoric (even Brian DePalma sneaked into a screening just for fun) to appalled. In his hotel room later that day, director Ferrara appeared to be bouncing off the walls, but evidently that's just his natural personality. He claims he didn't have a clear idea of what he was going to have the girls do in that scene, and that it was Keitel who had asked his director to trust him and let the cameras roll. "I didn't even know what he was going to do until he did it," says Ferrara. "Harvey was going through a tough time in his personal life, and who knew what he was going to come up with next."

The tough time refers to his protracted breakup with wife Lorraine Bracco, who had left him for Edward James Olmos, whom she later married. The custody battle over their daughter dragged on after that. It turns out that the girl who feigns oral sex in the car had been Keitel and Bracco's baby-sitter. "You think Woody Allen is bad?" says Ferrara after being momentarily distressed that word has leaked out about the identity of the actress. "This was his live-in baby-sitter!" Ferrara slaps his head in mock agony.

"The girls had never acted, they just wanted to be in a movie, they said they were ready for anything, they could handle this guy," says Ferrara. "I left the camera running. I thought he was going to get in the car with them, but no, he stayed outside. Harvey is wild, he'll do anything."

Keitel and Ferrara didn't have their stories straight, because later that same day over a drink in the hotel lobby, Keitel insisted the masturbation scene was scripted.

But he takes credit for the full-frontal nude scene, saying it was his idea. "I would never do a gratuitous sex scene. The event dictates things," he says in an intense, focused way that makes him seem either like a priest or an axe murderer. "We are talking about a man's slide into hell, in terms of his self-

FILMOGRAPHY

Who's That Knocking at My Door?,
1968
Street Scenes 1970, (production
assistant) 1970
Mean Streets, 1973
Alice Doesn't Live Here Anymore,
1974
That's the Way of the World,
1975
Buffalo Bill and the Indians, 1976
Mother, Jugs & Speed, 1976
Taxi Driver, 1976
Welcome to L.A., 1976
The Duellists, 1977
Fingers, 1978
Blue Collar, 1978
Eagle's Wing, 1978
La Mort en direct, 1979
Bad Timing: A Sensual Obsession,
1980
Saturn 3, 1980
The Border, 1982
La Nuit de Varennes, 1982
Copkiller, 1983
Exposed, 1983
Nemo, 1983
Une Pierre dans la bouche, 1983
Falling in Love, 1984
Un complicato intrigo di donne,
vicoli e delitti, 1985
Off Beat, 1985
El caballero del Dragon, 1986
The Men's Club, 1986
Wise Guys, 1986
Blindside, 1987
Dear America, 1987
Hello, Actors Studio, 1987
L'Inchiesta, 1987
The Pick-Up Artist, 1987
Caro Gorbaciov, 1988
The January Man, 1988

denigration. There is nothing gratuitous in this movie, just the opposite is so. It is necessary to explore the nature of things, violence being one of those things, love being another. *Bad Lieutenant* is one of those adult discussions, the kind where you ask your children to leave the room."

But maybe not the baby-sitter.

Then came *The Piano*, a different story, certainly a different tone. New Zealand director Jane Campion made this intelligent, erotic movie with a small budget and harsh local conditions. Holly Hunter plays a prim, mute nineteenth-century mail-order bride who travels with her daughter and beloved piano to Sam Neill's New Zealand frontier cottage. Keitel is a white neighbor who has gone native, living comfortably but reclusively among the Maoris. He buys the piano from Neill, then sells it back to Hunter one black key at a time in exchange for piano "lessons"—which mostly consist of her playing while he looks up her skirts. Her playing stirs his passion, so much so that in one famous scene, he lovingly dusts the piano in the nude.

It also established Keitel as a man who'll do anything for art, even though the piano-dusting scene was conspicuously trimmed for ratings purposes between the time it was shown at the world's film festivals and its multi-Oscar-winning domestic release. Those few snipped frames are enough to nearly ruin Keitel's full-frontal reputation.

Proving that an actor's ability to titillate can rise or fall depending on how a director and cinematographer make them look, Keitel and costar Madonna suffer as sex objects in *Dangerous Game*.

The Last Temptation of Christ,
1988
Two Evil Eyes, 1990
The Two Jakes, 1990
Mortal Thoughts, 1991
Thelma & Louise, 1991
Bugsy, 1991
Bad Lieutenant, 1992
Reservoir Dogs, 1992
Sister Act, 1992
Point of No Return, 1993
Rising Sun, 1993
Dangerous Game, 1993
Monkey Trouble, 1994
Pulp Fiction, 1994
Clockers, 1995
Somebody to Love, 1995

Nicole Kidman

"Nic" at Night

In the U.S., Nicole Kidman is still more famous for having married TOM CRUISE than for her films. But in Australia, where her parents moved her from Hawaii when she was an infant, she is a member of acting royalty, along with MEL GIBSON, Judy Davis, and Bryan Brown. During a tour of that country sponsored in 1992 by the Australian Film Institute, every native thespian spoke adoringly (and carefully!) of "Nic"—not only because she seems to have left behind good feelings, but because there isn't an actor down under who wouldn't like a piece of the Nic success story.

The red-headed actress, born in 1967, studied ballet and acting as a child, appearing at age four in a Nativity play and making her professional stage debut at ten. She made her first film at fourteen.

The minute she was seen in Phillip Noyce's *Dead Calm* (1989) being menaced aboard a yacht by psycho interloper Billy Zane, she was assured of an American career. She starred opposite racecar driver Tom Cruise in *Days of*

Thunder (1990) as cool-beauty brain surgeon, Claire Lewicki. Claire's job was to attend to Cruise's throbbing head; off-screen, the throbbing was moving downward toward the heart (or even lower) because the couple got married later that year. Never mind that at twenty-three and with a mass of carefully tended red ringlets, she didn't seem a bit like a brain surgeon.

Despite her chaste scenes with husband Tom Cruise in *Far and Away*, Nicole Kidman doffs her clothes casually in other movies, which can either reassure or unnerve viewers.

FILMOGRAPHY

BMX Bandits, 1983
Bush Christmas, 1983
Wills and Burke—The Untold
Story, 1985
Windrider, 1986
The Bit Part, 1987
Watch the Shadows Dance, 1988
Dead Calm, 1989
Emerald City, 1989
Days of Thunder, 1990
Flirting, 1990
Billy Bathgate, 1991
Far and Away, 1992
Malice, 1993
My Life, 1993
Portrait of a Lady, 1995
To Die For, 1995

There would be better roles to come.

Although *Dead Calm* had a bit of nudity, *Billy Bathgate* (1991) went all out with Kidman as a sexy mob moll who casually strips in front of a visitor and a three-way mirror. Her absolute aplomb about going au naturel is what creates tension, erotic and otherwise, in the viewer.

She was very chaste in *Far and Away* (1992)—surprisingly, since it costarred her husband. Then, she had some explicit and what turns out to be nasty sex in the twisty thriller *Malice* (1993), in a juicy role as a kindergarten teacher who goes to unbelievable lengths to get what she wants. The reason the sex is nasty is that when we first see her masterfully astride gentle hubby Bill Pullman, after sharing Chinese food from a carton, it seems like a loving after-dinner treat. When we know her character a bit better, the sex in retrospect isn't much of a turn-on.

Kidman reprises her *Malice* persona in the black comedy *To Die For* (1995), where she plays a suburban wife with a unique sense of timing. While going down on teenager Joaquin Phoenix, she asks him to do her a big favor—to kill off hubby Matt Dillon.

What adds spice to Kidman's chameleonlike character in *Malice* and *To Die For* is the public's faint distrust of the motivations behind her marriage. Any time a lesser known actor marries a star, there is a certain amount of skepticism—is it true love, or a career move?

It turns out that Kidman's acting abilities surpass the need to trade on her husband's name. Still, his clout probably helps Kidman weed out the gratuitous roles an actress with her doll-perfect looks would fall heir to; it is possible her powerful marital status affords her choices many actresses don't have. The daughter of a biochemist and an educator, Kidman isn't aiming for a career as window dressing, even if she may never convince us she's a brain surgeon.

Julianne Moore

"Why Does Naked Make It Art?"

A fter director Robert Altman's Hollywood career resurrection with *The Player* (1992), everyone was once again eager to appear in his ensemble movies. Yet, not everyone was crazy about taking the role of Marian Wyman, painter of nudes, in 1993's *Short Cuts*. Julianne Moore eventually took the gamble of appearing bottomless, and it paid off.

"My paintings are about seeing and the responsibility that comes with it," Marian tells an art dealer in the movie. There's plenty to see in *Short Cuts*, and the responsibility ultimately falls on the actors. The singer Huey Lewis appears to whip it out to take a leak during a fishing expedition, but what he whips out is really a porn-store rubber dildo with a water tube attached. Lori Singer is spied upon by the pool cleaner as she strips, jumps in, and does the Dead Man's Float as preparation for the real thing.

But the scene most talked about in this collection of intertwined Raymond Carver stories is when Marian, having spilled white wine on her

109

In *Short Cuts*, the short and curlies are front and center in Julianne Moore's big confrontation with husband Matthew Modine over an old marital indiscretion.

white gauzy skirt moments before guests are due, conducts a full-scale marital argument with husband Matthew Modine while immodest from the waist down.

Moore, a graduate of the Boston University School for the Performing Arts, won a 1988 Emmy for playing twins, Sabrina and Frannie Hughes, on the soap *As the World Turns* before making her theatrical film debut in *Tales From the Darkside: The Movie*. She had a memorable supporting role in *The Hand That Rocks the Cradle* (1992) as Annabella Sciorra's bitchy, outspoken best friend Marlene. In that movie, she's on to psycho nanny Rebecca De Mornay before anyone else, and finds that those who visit glass greenhouses shouldn't cast stones.

In 1993, Moore had a small part as a doctor suspicious of "orderly" Harrison Ford in *The Fugitive*.

Then, *Short Cuts* opened the 1993 New York Film Festival, and *tout* Hollywood was talking about the guts it took to perform an extended dramatic scene sans shorts. The painter Marian washes and blow-dries her soiled skirt while raging at the husband who wants to know whether she ever kissed another man some years back after a party. Moore's thatch of red pubic hair in the center of the screen—upon which all eyes are unquestionably focused—becomes a blunt visual cue to the outcome of the argument. It turns out kissing wasn't all she did on the night in question.

Lower frontal female nudity is rare in American movies, especially starring known actresses. Altman's decision to shoot the scene with the camera positioned that way can be interpreted as audacious, funny, insulting, or downright meanspirited, depending on how you feel about the movie (or about Altman, who is famous for having his actresses disrobe). As Modine says earlier when considering Marian's paintings, "Why does naked make it art?"

FILMOGRAPHY

Tales From the Darkside, 1990
The Hand That Rocks the Cradle, 1992
The Gun in Betty Lou's Handbag, 1992
Body of Evidence, 1993
Benny & Joon, 1993
The Fugitive, 1993
Short Cuts, 1993
Vanya on 42nd Street, 1994

Theresa Russell
She Mates and She Kills—But First a Little Undressing

To put it kindly, Theresa Russell is an acquired taste. There are those who think she can't act a lick.

Then there's her husband, Nicolas Roeg. Obviously, *he* thinks she can act. He casts her in most of his movies, and with his cinematographer's eye—the first movie he ever worked on was as a camera operator for *Lawrence of Arabia*—he at least recognizes his wife's visual appeal, which is considerable.

Even those (ahem) who think Russell can't act a lick still cut her some slack for *Bad Timing: A Sensual Obsession* (1980), her first movie with Roeg. Russell plays Milena, a bad girl on a downward spiral, and Art Garfunkel (of all people) plays a shrink who becomes totally and destructively obsessed with her. Necrophilia, anyone?

One of Russell's full-frontal nude scenes in this movie is interspersed with footage of a tracheotomy operation. The normally terse Craig Hosoda comments about this scene in his *Bare Facts Video Guide*: "Kind of gross."

Gross, perhaps, but a brilliant, disturbing movie nonetheless. (And what could be more disturbing than sex scenes with an actor as unappealing as Garfunkel?) The movie is still not out on video due to copyright problems in its native England.

Russell was born Theresa Paup in San Diego, in 1957. She studied acting at the Lee Strasberg Theater Institute in Hollywood, making her debut in Elia Kazan's *The Last Tycoon* (1976), a star-studded bomb.

Russell married Roeg in 1985, had two sons, and continued to shed her clothes on occasion, including in the movie she is most famous for in the U.S., Bob Rafelson's *Black Widow* (1986). The tag line for the movie went: "She mates and she kills," because Russell played a career widow named

Theresa Russell gives a preview of some of her talents for the title role of *Whore*, one of a career full of movies in which she demonstrates similar gifts.

Like many actors whose bodies are often the most memorable parts of their performance, Russell is as comfortable strutting her stuff off-screen as on it.

Photo courtesy of Albert Ferreira/DMI

FILMOGRAPHY

The Last Tycoon, 1976
Straight Time, 1978
Bad Timing: A Sensual Obsession, 1980
Eureka, 1982
The Razor's Edge, 1984
Insignificance, 1985
Aria, 1987
Black Widow, 1987
Track 29, 1987
Physical Evidence, 1988
Impulse, 1990
Whore, 1991
Kafka, 1991
Cold Heaven, 1992
Being Human (narrator), 1993

Catherine who stalked, married, then offed wealthy men. Her appeal was wider than that, since Justice Department investigator Debra Winger falls into the web as well, with some homoerotic tension between the two leading ladies.

If you think Roeg is a weird director, how about Ken Russell? In 1991, Theresa—no relation—poured herself into a leather micromini with a provocative zipper right up the back seam to play the lead in *Whore*, a movie that makes the not very startling argument that streetwalking is a hell of a way to make a living. Russell's flat voice-over narration doesn't help. The only thing the movie advances is Russell's oeuvre of nude scenes.

Eric Stoltz

Dream on

Sometime during 1994, Eric Stoltz began displaying a seemingly pathological need to be the Gene Hackman of his generation, appearing in as many movies as he could fit into his schedule. At the same time, he began displaying more of himself than perhaps was necessary.

Maybe it was the movie *Haunted Summer* (1988) that motivated him to let it all hang out. There, the thoroughly modern Los Angeleno played the poet Percy Bysshe Shelley during that fateful, historical, star-studded slumber party (Lord Byron was there, too), the one after which this then-girlfriend, Mary Godwin, wrote *Frankenstein*. Sleepovers with literary lights can be so amusing, so productive.

And so naked. The poet Shelley takes a shower under a waterfall for all to see, perhaps the better to get his creative juices flowing.

With this as precedent, it shouldn't have been a complete surprise when the movie *Naked in New York* (1994) made good on its title—in a pretentious

FILMOGRAPHY

Fast Times at Ridgemont High,
1982
Running Hot, 1984
Surf II, 1984
The Wild Life, 1984
Code Name Emerald, 1985
Mask, 1985
The New Kids, 1985
Lionheart, 1987
Sister, Sister, 1987
Some Kind of Wonderful, 1987
Haunted Summer, 1988
Manifesto, 1988
The Fly II, 1989
Say Anything, 1989
Memphis Belle, 1990
Money, 1991
The Waterdance, 1991
Singles, 1992
Bodies, Rest & Motion (also producer), 1993
Naked in New York, 1994
Killing Zoe, 1994
Sleep With Me, 1994
Pulp Fiction, 1994
Little Women, 1994
Fluke, 1995
Rob Roy, 1995

kind of way—by having lead actor Stoltz show "vulnerability" by experiencing a dream sequence in which he is bare, head to toe.

"What is the big deal with nudity?" he rhetorically asked of *Movieline* magazine. "When I see a love scene where the actors are strategically covered, I think, 'There's an actor who's uncomfortable being nude, and [he] shouldn't have taken the role.'"

Stoltz wasn't uncomfortable with his state of undress, although his pale, freckled skin and orange locks aren't everyone's cup of tea. "Don't you get sick of seeing actors who are in shape?" he complained. "I must say I get a little bored seeing actors who have really great bodies, and actresses with perfect measurements. I'm becoming more interested in odd shapes and imperfections."

Nevertheless, Stoltz says that doing the scene, to which the nudity was added as an afterthought on the day of shooting, made him "more uncomfortable than anything else I had to do. There was a female director of photography, a female assistant, and a female focus puller. You feel sized-up enough when they're taking focus marks and measuring the lens."

Stoltz was born in Whittier, California, on September 21, 1961, and moved to Santa Barbara at age eight. After an early interest in music (he studied trumpet and piano), he applied himself to theater for two years at the University of Southern California at Los Angeles, traveling to the Edinburgh Festival in Scotland as part of a repertory company.

He made his debut in *Fast Times at Ridgemont High* (1982), *on which* he so ridiculed Nicolas Coppola that the fellow first-timer subsequently dropped his famous uncle's last name and thereafter was known as Nicolas Cage. It was also around this time that Stoltz lost his virginity to Ally Sheedy, a fact he offered an interviewer only so that he wouldn't have to talk about his real source of interest, girlfriend Bridget Fonda. It was on *Fast Times* that he also met costar JENNIFER JASON

LEIGH, with whom he had a relationship.

Stoltz made his mark early on in *Mask* (1985) as Cher's horribly disfigured son, then missed out on a golden opportunity when he was cast as Marty McFly in *Back to the Future* (1985) and then fired after three weeks' work to make way for Michael J. Fox. Then, it was not until 1991's *The Waterdance* as a paraplegic adjusting to his fate that he was solid in a quality adult production again (with a naked Helen Hunt giving him a little personal physical therapy in his hospital bed).

In *Sleep With Me* (1994), he wound up in a silly love triangle with Meg Tilly at the center; that movie was written in sections by six different screenwriter pals, and it shows in the unevenness of their contributions. (One was Neal Jimenez of *The Waterdance*, which explains the Stoltz connection.)

Naked in New York premiered the same year that saw Stoltz popping up in *Sleep With Me, Killing Zoe, Pulp Fiction*, and *Little Women*. Of course, having Stoltz unburden himself of his trousers in a year that the actor was so omnipresent gives *Naked in New York* a higher place in the firmament of memory than it deserves.

Eric Stoltz and Meg Tilly under the sheets make two thirds of the love triangle in *Sleep With Me*.

Bruce Willis

No Body Doubles, Please

On a breezy night on the Riviera in May 1994, something was unveiled that never had been seen before—at least, not by most of several hundred people in attendance. It was Bruce Willis's penis, magnified beyond its usual proportions by being projected onto a giant movie screen.

"We have confidence in our bodies," announced Willis after the unveiling, as he and willowy *Color of Night* costar Jane March faced a crowd of journalists at the Cannes Film Festival. The brief press conference capped a sneak preview of scenes that would not be seen in the movie's U.S. theatrical distribution by Hollywood Pictures, a division of family-oriented Disney. This stuff was way too hot for an R rating, the boundary that the studio is contractually not allowed to exceed.

This *Color* is indeed colorful. Willis and March make love in a pool.

....

Bruce Willis had his personal gym flown in during the making of *Die Hard 3* because he realizes that his well-developed upper body is as integral to the John McClane character as his sarcastic line delivery.

....

March, every inch of whose body is familiar to fans of *The Lover*, travels down Willis's loins, down beneath the water line, down, down, down, until she is about to go down on Willis's willy, which actually grazes her cheek due to the unscheduled undulation of the water.

"Sex scenes are so uncomfortable to do," argued Willis that night, although he looked pretty sanguine up there on the screen. Must be a testament to his acting abilities. "So much of the work is about what you're *not* seeing. It's so technical."

A radio reporter from Philadelphia cut the press conference short by asking Willis, to scattered applause and boos, how he can justify taking money for making "this shit."

"That's an asshole thing to say," replied Willis testily before stomping off the stage.

History would bear out the radio reporter's concerns— *Color of Night* met with wilting reviews. But later the night of the preview, far from the madding crowd, Willis is relaxing aboard the well appointed yacht of the movie's producer, Andrew Vajna. The yacht has wall-to-wall carpeting and a working fireplace, although the Riviera in May is hardly the place to light up. Under these circumstances—with a big cigar dangling from his mouth, lounging in Italian loafers and no socks, being presented with choice items from the buffet and surrounded by bodyguards, agents, and old friends who travel with him in a pack—Willis is more amenable to discussing matters of the skin.

"I don't understand all the hoopla about full-frontal nudity," he says. "I don't have hang-ups about it. We didn't use body doubles. All the nudity is in the context of the story, not just for the sake of me being naked. It's like wearing a costume or makeup."

Or, *not* wearing a costume or makeup, to be more precise.

"In America we're hung up about telling people what they should do. I find it amusing that so much attention has been focused on the nudity, I guess because it helps sell the movie.

It gives people something to talk about."

Willis was born in West Germany on March 19, 1955, then raised from the age of two in Penns Grove, New Jersey. He is one of Manhattan's most famous former bartenders because of his stints at Cafe Central and Kamikaze.

The television series *Moonlighting* made him a star for his double entendre bantering with Cybill Shepherd, but his movie career was founded on the smirking heroics of John McClane in the amiable, glass-shattering *Die Hard* series. His fans don't like it when he strays too far from the formula—he didn't even have any love scenes until *Striking Distance* in 1993 with Sarah Jessica Parker—and of course, the bombs *Hudson Hawk* (1991) and *The Bonfire of the Vanities* (1990) didn't help. Rumors of trouble in his marriage to DEMI MOORE surface any time one of them threatens to become more bankable than the other.

Hot young director Quentin Tarantino knew exactly how

Willis and Jane March in a state of quiescence after she goes down on him underwater in *Color of Night*. No body doubles for them, thank you.

FILMOGRAPHY

Blind Date, 1987
Die Hard, 1988
Sunset, 1988
In Country, 1989
Look Who's Talking (voice), 1989
That's Adequate, 1989
The Bonfire of the Vanities, 1990
Die Hard 2: Die Harder, 1990
Look Who's Talking Too (voice), 1990
Billy Bathgate, 1991
Hudson Hawk, 1991
The Last Boy Scout, 1991
Mortal Thoughts, 1991
Death Becomes Her, 1992
The Player, 1992
National Lampoon's Loaded Weapon 1, 1993
Striking Distance, 1993
Color of Night, 1994
North, 1994
Pulp Fiction, 1994
Die Hard With a Vengeance, 1995
12 Monkeys, 1995
Dollar for the Dead, 1995
Four Rooms, 1995

to use Willis to best advantage in *Pulp Fiction* (1994). Willis plays a boxer who throws a fight and is about to escape with the dough and his girlfriend when he remembers a memento he left behind. On his way to retrieve it, he is sucked into a wild nightmare of crossed loyalties and medieval sex torture; he gets himself out of that scrape the way John McClane might. Willis has a few artfully shot nude scenes—in bed with his girlfriend, coming out of the shower—so that his toned, buffed body is teasingly on display without jeopardizing the R rating.

Willis is popular not only for being semitough, but for being semiclad. It's not just that he saves an entire high-rise office building in the first *Die Hard*, but he does it in his undershirt and bare feet. There is something stripped-down about his character in every respect, as if he represents the mythic ideal of American can-do, the guy who has nothing, requires nothing, and is ingenious at making something out of nothing. When Willis shot the third *Die Hard* in New York in the summer of 1994, he asked that his personal gym be flown in, because his trapezius muscles are as integral to that character as his smart mouth.

That is one reason why *Color of Night* was such a washout for Willis. He plays a guilt-ridden shrink whose last patient jumped out of his window and splattered herself all over the pavement. On his path to healing, he must solve the murder of a colleague while having rejuvenating sex with the mysterious March. Outside of a few sweaty jogging scenes and the ultimately snipped sex scenes, there was no call in the script for Willis to disrobe. The way Superman needs to duck into a phone booth and change into uniform, Willis needs an excuse to strip down for action.

Color of Night opened in the U.S. to hoots of derision. The sex scenes were all stanched with tourniquet editing. The swimming pool number is one of several that fades out creamily just when things are getting good.

Naked Ambition

STARS WHO DISROBE AT THE DROP
OF A HAT, OR WHATEVER

William Baldwin

Steamy Sex on a Sliver Platter

With a name like Baldwin, it was perhaps inevitable that William, brother of hunky fellow exhibitionists Daniel, Stephen, and ALEC BALDWIN, would become a sex symbol. To ensure it wasn't only in the hands of fate, William groomed himself for the job, taking only those roles that would showcase his exceptional body, and hoping that fame of a more enduring nature would follow.

Early morning dog walkers on Manhattan's East Side often catch Baldwin returning home from a night out, his slicked-back hair suggestively tousled. That's his appeal—the suggestion of someone who can go all night and, like the Energizer bunny, keep on going.

Originally a successful model whose bare torso could sell any product,

Baldwin's tousled, casual appearance gives viewers the impression he's up for anything, any time—and since he looks the same way off-screen, they may be right.

Photo courtesy of Alex Oliveira/DMI

William—Billy to loved ones—began his movie career on the fast track to sexual stardom. He played an unhappy stud in *Flatliners* (1990), who could only have sex, sex, sex, but never long enough to make an emotional commitment. While the other characters in the movie were busy experimenting with near-death experiences (i.e., "flatlining"), Baldwin was concerning himself with *le petit mort*, and videotaping himself in the act, the Rob Lowe route to sexual immortality.

The next time Baldwin made a movie, the hype machine promised that it would make him a star. But the real star of *Backdraft* (1991) turned out to be the special effects that made the orange tongues of three-alarm fires look sexy. It's true that Baldwin took a soapy shower butt-to-butt with fellow firefighter Jason Gedrick, but the emphasis in *Backdraft* shifted improbably to family melodrama. Maybe the shower scene was the best director Ron Howard could do under the circumstances, because he spent much effort adjusting the lighting and camera angles so that Baldwin's narrow-set features didn't make him look cross-eyed, a less than enticing effect that can happen when Baldwin is photographed indifferently.

Baldwin didn't give up on his dream of being a sex symbol. Like Alex, his screen persona is exhibitionistic and narcissistic enough to appeal equally to men and women; funny that those are qualities that inhibit relationships in real life yet encourage the fantasy of intimacy when at a cinematic remove.

In a return to the carnal preoccupations of his character in *Flatliners*, Baldwin plays a workaholic stud hired to romance and jilt a woman's lesbian lover in *Three of Hearts* (1993), only to fall in live with her himself.

Stuck in the shadow (no pun intended) of older brother Alec, William was having trouble getting a leg up on showbiz. What he needed was a role that would catapult him into leading-man status. It looked like he had finally found the right break with *Sliver* (1993), which was to be a hot suspense story set in a Manhattan high-rise populated mostly by newly dead women and the great-looking guys who may have thrown them head over heels over a balcony. Costar SHARON STONE was just coming off her incredible no-panty success of *Basic Instinct*, and the pairing, if it worked, could have made Baldwin just as bankable.

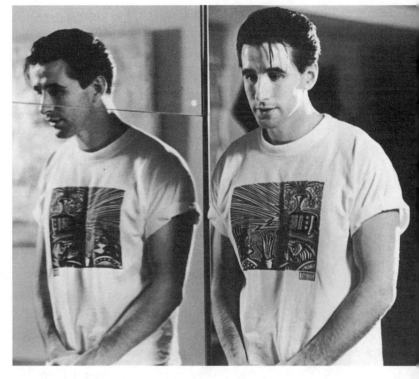

The movie, based on the sexy Ira Levin murder mystery, has Stone playing a magazine editor who is dating two men in her building, either of whom could be planning to give her a fatal kiss-off. The identity of the murderer was changed from the original ending of the book in order to throw informed viewers off the scent. Baldwin plays what must be New York's youngest, cutest, and most accessible landlord, which is hard to take seriously. But that he is also a potentially Tony Perkins–style psycho was hardly a career booster.

William Baldwin hits the gym in *Sliver*, where he gets off on watching himself working out in the mirror. That's just about as hot as it gets after the movie dropped Baldwin's full-frontal scenes to facilitate an R rating.

As for the sex and nudity the movie had promised, only some of it wound up on the screen. *Sliver* flirted for a while with the dreaded NC–17 rating, which must be why so many of the hormonal scenes between Baldwin and Stone look as if they were abandoned prematurely in an attempt to cool the jets of the MPAA's ratings board. The roiling volcano ending

FILMOGRAPHY

Flatliners, 1990
Internal Affairs, 1990
Backdraft, 1991
The Last Party, 1993
Three of Hearts, 1993
Sliver, 1993
Fair Game, 1995

that was shot at great expense and danger and then never used is an apt metaphor for how Baldwin's libidinous screen personality was tamed in the interests of a conservative ratings approach. And all sightings of William's bald one have been excised.

Some of the scenes that remain are further encumbered by the lack of chemistry between the two stars. At one point, Baldwin comes at Stone from behind, against a marble pillar, but in later interviews, Baldwin implied that the marble pillar was not the only thing stonelike about shooting that scene.

It is a testament to Baldwin's talent for screen narcissism that his most prurient scene is when he worships his own sweaty muscles in the mirror during a workout in the building's health club. This is because *Sliver* is a movie that prefers the appearance of things to the reality of them; so much for the movie's promise of good, hot sex. Its theme of voyeurism is a subject beloved by directors, who spend a good deal of their lives peering through lenses. Unfortunately for the audience, voyeurism is a passive hobby, on top of which movie-watching is already a passive experience.

Director Phillip Noyce, who once made an excellent, quiet little thriller called *Dead Calm*, is about as subtle here as the perniciously phallic imagery—the sliver building itself, which pokes suggestively into the air like the trademark of a singles club, or the half-eaten eclair on Stone's plate right after she has her first postdivorce orgasm, or the model volcano that is an integral part of Baldwin's apartment decor and which was meant to anticipate the now-discarded ending. Too bad his apartment is on the thirteenth floor; *Sliver* could have been so lucky for his career.

More nude scenes are doubtless in this Baldwin's future. In 1995, he teamed with that noted thespian Cindy Crawford for *Fair Game*; it's fair game to say it might be a race to see whose clothes are unfastened first.

Bo Derek

Forever a 10, But Never Much More

"Who wants to see a Bo Derek movie where she doesn't take her clothes off?" once asked the discomfitingly candid John Derek about his wife, his own private pinup queen.

Derek discovered Mary Cathleen Collins on a Mykonos beach in 1973 and put the teenager in the movie he was shooting, *Fantasies.* Then, he added her to his string of look-alike wives—Ursula Andress, Linda Evans—and they've been together ever since. While Bo molds her body through exercise, John has molded her image through movie projects and several *Playboy* spreads.

The text accompanying the pictorial gives one pause; it turns out that Bo cuts the fat off John's steak even in public. Obviously, the couple's mutual dependence goes deeper than anyone knows.

But the photos—taken as usual by John—are magnificent, revealing a still-perfect body that has been sculpted especially for the camera, with that

FILMOGRAPHY

Fantasies, 1983
Orca, The Killer Whale, 1977
10, 1979
A Change of Seasons, 1980
Tarzan, The Ape Man, 1981
Bolero, 1984
Ghosts Can't Do It, 1990
Hot Chocolate, 1992
Tommy Boy, 1995

curiously concave belly for which John designs special poses.

With the exception of *10*, the 1979 movie that made Bo and her cornrows indelible as the perfect woman of Dudley Moore's dreams, Bo's film outings have been ultraserious (and therefore campy) exercises in soft-core eroticism. Whether it be the Tarzan story rehashed (*Tarzan, The Ape Man*, 1981) or the tale of a coed combing exotic locales for the right man to deflower her (*Bolero*, 1984), Derek's movies all have one thing in common—numerous plot devices whereby the heroine will be prettily photographed in the raw. She does, however, have the dubious distinction of sharing a nude hot tub scene with Anthony Hopkins in *A Change of Seasons* (1980).

The Derek couple's zest to unzip Bo has given her an enduring fame of a kind, but kept her from any sort of acting challenges, thus limiting the types of roles she could handle. She is at her most animated when she is captured in still-life photographs.

Jennifer Jason Leigh

Sex as Primal-Scream Therapy

Jennifer Jason Leigh describes herself as the classic good little girl when she was growing up. She gets to act out her bad side in movies, gravitating to slutty, trampy roles, girls who look for love in all the wrong places.

Born in 1962, tiny and with pale, fragile-looking skin, she still has the baby-fat innocence of an adolescent combined with the angry sneer of a runaway. Her nude scenes aren't langorous excursions into sensuality, but more like the sexual equivalent of primal-scream therapy, intense and traumatic.

In *Last Exit to Brooklyn* (1990), she's a platinum-blond, frizzy-haired prostitute with an aching need for attention that results in her being gang-raped. In *Single White Female* (1992), she has such a needy crush on roommate Bridget Fonda that she masturbates while thinking about her, then seduces Fonda's boyfriend (the oral sex was much more explicit before the movie was trimmed for release; you actually saw Leigh's lips sticky and dripping after the deed).

In *Short Cuts* (1993), Leigh drew laughs as a new mother who works from home, talking dirty for a phone sex line. She instructs her clients in the ways of bondage and discipline with a no-nonsense direct-ness. "I'm going to introduce your *dick* to my *tonsils*," she announces, cradling the phone with her shoulder so that she can feed the baby and do some housework at the same time.

"I won't do anything that I feel is exploitive, that doesn't tell you something about the character or move the story forward," says Leigh of choosing her roles.

In a tour de force as the witty but terminally despairing writer and theater critic Dorothy Parker in *Mrs. Parker and the Vicious Circle* (1994), Leigh has frequent (nonexplicit) sex with a succession of ill-advised partners. She hauls one partner off into the bushes after just meeting him, then stumbles back drunkenly moments later. "Don't worry," she tells him. "I don't review rehearsals."

Leigh has been partly or totally starkers in several of her movies, but maybe her scenes can never compare with what she and her friends dreamed up in high school. "We girls used to write really raunchy erotic stories for each other. They had the most explicit sex scenes you've ever read. They're funny to read now, but at the time we all thought they were pretty sexy."

FILMOGRAPHY

Eyes of a Stranger, 1980
Fast Times at Ridgemont High, 1982
Wrong Is Right, 1982
Easy Money, 1983
Grandview, U.S.A., 1984
Flesh and Blood, 1985
The Hitcher, 1986
The Men's Club, 1986
Under Cover, 1987
Sister, Sister, 1988
The Big Picture, 1989
Heart of Midnight, 1989
Last Exit to Brooklyn, 1989
Miami Blues, 1990
Backdraft, 1991
Crooked Hearts, 1991
Rush, 1991
Single White Female, 1992
Short Cuts, 1993
The Hudsucker Proxy, 1994
Mrs. Parker and the Vicious Circle, 1994
Delores Claiborne, 1995

(Above) Jennifer Jason Leigh as the needy prostitute of *Last Exit to Brooklyn*, one of a collection of trampy roles she has specialized in.

Madonna

More Exposure Per Square Inch

Madonna naked, having group sex, being smeared with ritual blood— is it her latest movie? Her newest music vidclip?

Actually, that's Madonna in *A Certain Sacrifice*, a terrible 1981 student film she made in return for a month's rent when she was down and out in New York, before fame turned her into a one-woman publicity mill.

There's nothing so kinky in *A Certain Sacrifice* that she wouldn't try it again later. After all, this is a woman who has worn cone-shaped bras, feigned masturbation with religious artifacts, and slunk all over Warren Beatty in *Dick Tracy* while singing "I Always Get My Man" in a scene artfully lit to reveal she is wearing no underwear under her outerwear (with Madonna, it is difficult to tell undies from outies).

She got her man, although it's easy to see why she lost him in *Truth or Dare*, the documentary about Madonna in which she is shown ordering around her real-life lover Beatty, taunting him by calling him "pussy man,"

Madonna promises she always gets her man as torch singer Breathless Mahoney in *Dick Tracy*. In fact, she did get her man—she and costar (and director) Warren Beatty were breathless together on and off the set.

and then not understanding why he doesn't return her calls or want to be seen faithfully by her side for the camera.

Madonna Louise Ciccone was born August 16, 1959, in Detroit. As her music has matured, her melancholy ballads about the breakup with Sean Penn have turned to frankly erotic come-ons, full of orgasmic or breathy background vocals. To complement the confessional quality of her music, Madonna has increasingly revealed more in her acting—more of her body, anyway.

The media and the world were already tiring of her exhibitionism when she took on the role of suspected man-killer Rebecca Carlson in *Body of Evidence*. Here, she is formally accused of being a lethal weapon; presumably, she is so good in bed that men who have her have heart attacks as well. WILLEM DAFOE plays her gullible lawyer, who, perhaps in the interests of full disclosure, goes to bed with her to see what it's like.

Actually, he doesn't go to bed with her, at least not in the strict sense of the expression. They have sex in a variety of greatly uncomfortable situations, using hot wax and glass shards as aphrodisiacs. Dafoe's wife figures out he's cheating not from the usual telltale signs like hotel receipts, but from bruises, cuts, and blood stains.

Like Madonna, director Abel Ferrara's art often reflects his life. So, it was not such a stretch that he cast Madonna in his 1993 clinker *Dangerous Game*, about a director whose latest

project blurs the distinction between film and real life. Blurring it further is that Madonna is cast as a bad actress, and she isn't even good in a role seemingly tailor-made for her.

Because the movie, looking like it was made on a kitchen-sink budget, is supposed to make you doubt what is fact or fiction, the sequence where Madonna's costar goes too far in an anal rape scene makes the viewer uncomfortable, as if maybe it actually happened on the *Dangerous Game* set. But curiosity over this movie was at an all-time low among the dozen or so people who actually saw it in theaters.

"It was empowering for me to take my clothes off and then to put my clothing back on and go home and carry on with my day and not feel like I lost any dignity or self-esteem," Madonna told *Allure* magazine about being an artist's

Known for having often worn her underwear as outerwear, Madonna here forgoes both types of apparel for the amusement of Jean-Paul Gaultier, who designed those cone bras for her Blonde Ambition tour.

Photo courtesy Kevin of Winter/DMI

FILMOGRAPHY

A Certain Sacrifice, 1979
Desperately Seeking Susan, 1985
Vision Quest, 1985
At Close Range (song), 1986
Shanghai Surprise, 1986
Who's That Girl, 1987
Bloodhounds of Broadway, 1989
Dick Tracy, 1990
Truth or Dare (documentary), 1991
A League of Their Own, 1992
Shadows and Fog, 1992
Blast 'Em (documentary), 1992
Peter's Friends (newsreel footage), 1992
Body of Evidence, 1993
Dangerous Game, 1993
Four Rooms, 1995

model early in her career. "It made me think of my body as a work of art."

In case her public hadn't seen enough of that work of art—remember Rosie O'Donnell's line to her in *A League of Their Own*: "You think there are men in this country that ain't seen your bosoms?"—she then put out a coffee-table book of nude photos of herself called *Sex*, in which every inch of Madonna's flesh gets its fifteen minutes of fame.

By then, Madonna must have realized what the title *Dangerous Game* really referred to—the publicity game. She was overexposed on too many fronts. Even the David Letterman audience rejected her when she went on a cursing binge that had to be bleeped out. For damage control, she announced to an indifferent public that she would henceforth change her sexpot image to something more wholesome. In fact, it was her idea *not* to remove her top as called for by the script for *Four Rooms*, where she plays a witch. It just goes to show that nudity is titillating only to the point where the imagination still has something to play with.

(Above) Madonna (with Michael Jackson) covers up as much as she's capable of with silver lamé and fur.

Photo courtesy of David McGough/DMI

Demi Moore

Wearing the Body-Paint Birthday Suit

Has Demi Moore done more for the self-esteem of pregnant women than the Virgin Mary?

It's clear that the husky-voiced former model has always been comfortable with her body. Rubenesque with baby fat early in her career, she was nevertheless nude or topless in *Blame It on Rio* (1984), *About Last Night . . .* (1986), and *We're No Angels* (1989). On the New York stage, she made her Off-Broadway debut in the altogether in *The Early Girl*, running onstage clad only in a light dusting of pancake makeup before someone throws a towel over her.

She became the poster child for motherhood in 1991 with her infamous *Vanity Fair* cover, in which she managed to make full-term pregnancy look incredibly glamorous. With one hand resting on her breast, the other cradling her belly, Moore is totally bare and totally relaxed. The photo may have shocked or offended—some stores refused to sell or display the magazine—

but it actually prompted cultural acceptance of the pregnant female form in an age that prizes anorexia and prepubescence as fashion statements.

Ironically, Moore had a brief nude scene in the 1988 movie *The Seventh Sign*, in which she wore a pregnancy prosthetic. Marisa Tomei also wore a pregnancy prosthetic for a dimly lit nude shot in *The Paper* (1994); that the pregnancy was so prominently highlighted is most likely thanks to Moore's pioneer *Vanity Fair* cover. And the finale of Robert Altman's *Ready to Wear* (1994), in which a very genuinely pregnant model struts nakedly down a fashion runway, would have been more shocking had Moore not paved the way.

Moore also made the birthday suit her ensemble of choice in a subsequent *Vanity Fair* cover in which she wears nothing but a suit of body paint.

Demi Guynes was born November 11, 1962, in New Mexico, where she had what she has described in interviews as a turbulent childhood. She began her acting career on the soap opera *General Hospital*, then made a succession of pleasant, minor movies until her 1990 breakthrough in *Ghost*. In that Oscar-nominated movie, her makeup was never marred by the glycerine tears she shed for murdered boyfriend PATRICK SWAYZE, who comes back as a ghost to warn her of imminent danger and to assure her from beyond the grave that he will always love her. The scene in which bare-chested Swayze and Moore swoon over a spinning, gooey clay potter's wheel is a memorable pop-culture moment, parodied on *Saturday Night Live*, *Doogie Howser*,

Freshly showered, Demi Moore gets cold feet over moving in with Rob Lowe in *About Last Night . . .* Moore showed more earlier in her career to get it jump-started; later she used a body double in *Indecent Proposal* and never unclasped her bra in *Disclosure*.

M.D., and *Naked Gun 2 1/2: The Smell of Fear.*

By this time, Moore was eclipsing husband BRUCE WILLIS as the star in the family, which couldn't have been easy on their marriage. They costarred in *Mortal Thoughts* (1991), which Moore coproduced, where she was provocatively *intime* with Glenne Headley. *The Butcher's Wife* had Moore blond, sweet, and psychic, but fully clothed and not psychic enough to realize the movie would fizzle.

Moore was a starchy, no-nonsense military lawyer in *A Few Good Men* (1992); it seemed a shame to cast her next to fellow pretty-face TOM CRUISE and then not introduce a dalliance.

Indecent Proposal made it into everyone's cocktail party chatter in 1993. Moore plays the married woman to whom Robert Redford pays a million dollars for just for one night's pleasure. You'd think this would be an excellent opportunity for Moore to strip down to her *Vanity Fair* self, but when the big moment arrives on Redford's yacht, the two of them kiss and the scene fades out tactfully. Even Hollywood does not have the imagination to show us what million-dollar sex is supposed to look like. And it can't be blamed on the aging Redford's reluctance to do the scene, since Moore backed out of her sex scenes with movie husband Woody Harrelson as well and watched a body double go through the motions for her.

But sex can be worth even more than that when you take it to court, as MICHAEL DOUGLAS does to Moore in *Disclosure* (1994). "You just lie back and let me be the boss," says Moore as she unzips her underling's pants at eye-level, wielding her position of authority to get him into the sack. Suddenly modest, Moore never takes off her black bra, but her newly voluminous breasts swell from it so menacingly that she could easily have suffocated Douglas with them had she truly wanted to play out the movie's theme of sexual harassment.

Former model and soap actress Moore revels in the attentions of the camera.

Photo Courtesy of Albert Ferreira/DMI

FILMOGRAPHY

Choices, 1981
Parasite, 1982
Young Doctors in Love, 1982
Blame It on Rio, 1984
No Small Affair, 1984
St. Elmo's Fire, 1985
About Last Night ... , 1986
One Crazy Summer, 1986
Wisdom, 1986
The Seventh Sign, 1988
We're No Angels, 1989
Ghost, 1990
Nothing But Trouble, 1991
Mortal Thoughts (also coproducer), 1991
The Butcher's Wife, 1991
A Few Good Men, 1992
Indecent Proposal, 1993
Disclosure, 1994
The Gaslight Addition, 1995
The Juror, 1996

Sylvester Stallone

Mind Over Matter

Sylvester Stallone feels he's gotten a bum rap. While everyone acknowledges his chief rival, ARNOLD SCHWARZENEGGER, as a savvy businessman with a healthy sense of humor, Stallone is still ridiculed for his "Yo, Adrian" line delivery out of South Philadelphia. While Arnold is married to a classy Kennedy, Stallone has dated a succession of models after his messy breakup with Amazonian *Red Sonja* star Brigitte Nielsen. Stallone's own image of himself can be summed up by the nude pose he struck for the cover of *Vanity Fair*—Rodin's *The Thinker*.

The irony of that pose, however, is that Stallone can't shake the stigma of being considered all brawn and no brain (despite his Oscar triumph for *Rocky* in 1976). And probably because he really does revel in his own body, he has happily contributed to the public perception over the years. In 1970, he made the soft-core porn movie *A Party at Kitty and Stud's*, later retitled *The Italian Stallion* to cash in on the studmuffin's fame. In this early movie, Stallone has the thuggish look that Woody Allen later cast him for in *Bananas* to play a subway punk. But he doesn't yet have the muscle tone or body consciousness that helped make him an international action star. The only things protecting his modesty are a watch, a medallion on a chain, and the fact that he is uncircumcised.

For most of his subsequent career, Stallone would take any opportunity to show off his massive chest, whether it be crisscrossed with ammo belts or cinched with a boxer's prize belt. It is only since *Tango & Cash* in 1989 that he has toyed with nude scenes for the first time since his *Kitty and Stud* days. In *Tango & Cash*, he and archenemy KURT RUSSELL walk naked together into a prison shower and then spar over a fallen bar of soap to relieve some of the homoerotic tension that is integral to the buddy-movie genre. In *Rocky V* (1990) and the failed comedy *Stop! Or My Mom Will Shoot* (1992), there are literally half-assed shower scenes.

Demolition Man (1993) devised a clever new way for the increasingly self-revealing Stallone to display his carefully maintained body—it shows

By the time he made *Rambo III*, Stallone's body had swelled to meet the demands of his international action audience.

him climbing naked out of a tank where he has been cryogenically frozen into the future, much like MEL GIBSON's emergence in *Forever Young* (1992). As he nears fifty, Stallone is using his body to try to win respect for his mind.

"I think that people assume I'm some primordial being,

The Specialist showcases Stallone's veiny look, the result of low ratio of fat to muscle.

Stallone climbs out of the futuristic deep freeze totally naked in a bit of understandable movie preening in *Demolition Man*.

FILMOGRAPHY

A Party at Kitty and Stud's, 1970
Bananas, 1971
The Lords of Flatbush, 1974
Capone, 1975
Death Race 2000, 1975
Farewell, My Lovely, 1975
No Place to Hide, 1975
Cannonball, 1976
Rocky, 1976
F.I.S.T., 1978
Paradise Alley, 1978
Rocky II, 1979
Victory, 1981
Nighthawks, 1981
First Blood, 1982
Rocky III, 1982
Staying Alive (director), 1983
Rhinestone, 1984
Rambo: First Blood, Part II, 1985
Rocky IV, 1985
Cobra, 1986
Over the Top, 1987
Rambo III, 1988
Lock Up, 1989
Tango & Cash, 1989
Rocky V, 1990
Oscar, 1991
Stop! Or My Mom Will Shoot, 1992
Cliffhanger, 1993
Demolition Man, 1993
The Specialist, 1994
Judge Dredd, 1995

wallowing in a morass of mud and carrying a club on my shoulders. I don't think people understand that my life is much more cerebral than physical," Stallone has said.

His veiny, cut look clashed with SHARON STONE's shiny marble exterior in the shower lovemaking scenes of *The Specialist* (1994), proving that just because two people have their own personal trainers doesn't mean they're compatible.

Sharon Stone

No Panty Line

S haron Stone was just another looker in a town full of them until she uncrossed and recrossed her legs in *Basic Instinct* (1992). Not since Marilyn Monroe has there been such a stir over the no-panty look.

Her flash goes by in such a flash that it is very difficult to make out that it is indeed Stone's pubic hair that we are witnessing in the now-famous police interrogation scene, where the camera is on eye-level with her thighs. Stone is a possible murder suspect who is being outrageous in the third degree. Not only is she wearing no underwear, but she refuses to put out her cigarette—"What are ya gonna do, arrest me?"

Basic Instinct is a movie that bends over backward to titillate and shock. It opens with a woman using an ice pick to hack out the eye of her bound lover in some strange postcoital frenzy. If that doesn't put a cold glaze over the audience, the movie then segues to police headquarters for the "Look, Ma, No Panties" scene. There are other name-brand actresses who have proffered their

Sharon Stone gets a tongue-lashing from Michael Douglas in *Basic Instinct,* in which the two willingly demonstrate why Douglas calls her "the fuck of the century."

pubic region to the camera—Debra Winger in *The Sheltering Sky,* ELLEN BARKIN in *Siesta,* NICOLE KIDMAN in *Billy Bathgate,* JULIANNE MOORE in *Short Cuts.* But few offered the promise (unfulfilled, by the way) of opening their legs as well.

The beaver shot, by the way, goes by so quickly that only the very motivated have claimed to really see Stone's light brown thatch. But an Italian magazine made things easier by printing a blowup of a frame from the movie that proves beyond doubt that what went by in a flash was a flasher's delight.

Stone was born in Meadville, Pennsylvania, on March 10, 1958, and devoted her teen years to writing and studying drama, and winning beauty pageants. Back in 1975 when she was giving a dramatic reading of the Gettysburg Address at Meadville's annual Spring Festival Queen contest, young Sharon probably thought the world was her oyster.

It is her oyster now, although she doesn't always get to keep the pearls. The famous jeweler Harry Winston won a suit that Stone brought in which she claimed she didn't have to return an expensive choker after wearing it for publicity purposes. The case went to court, and no dice, no ice.

And no panties. Stone sans briefs is a hot commodity, even though her next two pantyless movies met with ridicule—*Sliver* (1993), in which she gyrates unconvincingly with WILLIAM BALDWIN in a Manhattan high-rise where women don't live long enough to pay their rent, and *The Specialist* (1994), in which Stone's shower scenes with fellow hardbody SYLVESTER STALLONE are a contest as to who can flex more impressively. (Stallone has the most veins, hands down.)

A former Ford model, Stone made her film debut as the "Pretty Girl on Train" in Woody Allen's *Stardust Memories* (1980), the symbol across the tracks of all the fun and hot times that Allen is missing in life. In a way, Stone is still the party-train girl, the sexpot who withholds just enough of her treasures to tease. The image has taken years to cultivate, as Stone didn't make much of an impression in her early string of films—unless you count how she managed to wear a nightgown in nearly every scene of Wes Craven's horror movie *Deadly Blessing* (1981), or the way her photojournalist character wears white pumps into the combat zone in *Year of the Gun* (1991).

She made a better impression kicking husband ARNOLD SCHWARZENEGGER in the nuts in *Total Recall* (1990), although her character got her comeuppance when the big guy shoots her dead and announces, "I'm getting a div*AWCE*." Stone is always better in roles where she kicks men in the balls; the problem with *Sliver* is that she was playing "vulnerable," and that's not what people want from her. They want the ice pick maiden, the woman who would not be at all offended to hear MICHAEL DOUGLAS describe her as "the fuck of the century."

After *Total Recall*, Stone did a calculated shoot for *Playboy*, which served as a valentine to casting agents. The spread paid off with *Basic Instinct*. "It was the most exciting and interesting and profoundly moving character I'd ever been offered," said

It's not just her lack of underwear but her lack of inhibition that makes Stone so appealing, plus the fact that she can segue effortlessly from jeans to elegant old-time glamour.

Photo courtesy of Albert Ferreira/DMI

148

Stone and Stallone have names and bodies that echo one another, but they failed to click in those arduous sex scenes of *The Specialist*.

FILMOGRAPHY

Stardust Memories, 1980
Deadly Blessing, 1981
Bolero (France), 1981
Irreconcilable Differences, 1984
King Solomon's Mines, 1985
Allan Quatermain and the Lost City of Gold, 1987
Action Jackson, 1988
Above the Law, 1988
Personal Choice (Beyond the Stars), 1989
Blood and Sand, 1989
Total Recall, 1990
He Said, She Said, 1991
Scissors, 1991
Year of the Gun, 1991
Basic Instinct, 1992
Where Sleeping Dogs Lie, 1992
Diary of a Hitman, 1992
Legends in Light (documentary), 1993
Sliver, 1993
Last Action Hero (cameo), 1993
Intersection, 1994
The Specialist, 1994
The Quick and the Dead (also coproducer), 1995
Casino, 1995
Last Dance, 1995

Stone rather high-mindedly at the 1992 Cannes Film Festival, where an extra forty-five seconds of missing sex scenes had just been restored for the more tolerant European market. "It's an example of the resurgence of strong parts for women in film. I never thought of myself personally as a 'sex babe,' but now that they're calling me that, I'm trying to just enjoy it and play with it."

The sex babe waxes intellectual about shooting those bondage clinches with costar Douglas. "To capture eroticism on camera is a very fragile thing," she explains, adding that the encounters were "very choreographed—they had to be because it was a lot of action, so to speak."

In her first western, *The Quick and the Dead* (1995), she's a tough gunslinger out for revenge. The Sam Raimi movie's chief mistake is to cut the sex scene between Stone and Leonardo Di Caprio. We see her waking up with an artfully draped nightshirt and feel cheated of seeing the carnal pleasures implied. Then, she's off her horse and back in the saddle with ROBERT DE NIRO when she plays a Las Vegas hooker in Martin Scorsese's *Casino*, a seventies period piece. Such is her stature, with or without heels, that Stone beat out both former porn star Traci Lords and MELANIE GRIFFITH for the coveted role. Her reward is to have sex scenes with, of all people, Joe Pesci—but only under threat of death.

Regrets Only

STARS WHO SHOULD HAVE KEPT THEIR CLOTHES ON

Dana Delany

Lights, Camera, Whips, Chains

Mistress Lisa is wearing a choke collar and a gold lamé bra, and she'll make you crawl like the worm that you are—back to the video store where you mistakenly rented *Exit to Eden* (1994).

Dana Delany makes a most unconvincing dominatrix at an island pleasure retreat for sadomasochists. It proves that no matter how lissome the body, not every actor is suited for portraying sexual perversion. Delany should have swum for her life and dignity back to *China Beach*, the television show on which she played that nice army nurse Colleen McMurphy from 1988 to 1991.

Delany was born March 13, 1956, in New York, and was one of the first females to graduate from the former male bastion of Phillips Academy pre-

Anxious to offset her good-girl image off-screen as well, Delany strikes a deliberate pose, well aware of its effect.

school in Andover. She studied drama at Wesleyan and worked the soap opera circuit (*Love of Life* and *As the World Turns*) before her Emmy-winning stint as Nurse McMurphy. The series kept her out of films for several years until *Housesitter* (1992), where she played the woman of architect Steve Martin's dreams before GOLDIE HAWN came along. There is a funny scene where Martin, trying surreptitiously to make a pass, walks his fingers stealthily up Delany's blouse, trying to do the "breaststroke."

After playing KURT RUSSELL's actress-lover in the failed Wyatt Earp saga *Tombstone* (1993), *Exit to Eden* was Delany's first shot at a leading role. She had to learn how to crack the whip, literally and figuratively. "Bathe me," she commands a willing if embarrassed Paul Mercurio. But you can't take her threats too seriously since Mistress Lisa is at heart a cream puff who perspires at her first glimpse of Mercurio shaking his bare buns so furiously that at movie theaters it seemed as if the projector would fly loose of its moorings.

Director Garry Marshall must have been having one of those Blake Edwards midlife crises. Not sure whether to titillate or amuse, to make a bold statement or retract one, his movie floats off like a lost bikini top. *Exit to Eden* doesn't have enough bondage detail for the discipline disciples, yet is too heavy on the hardware for fans of Marshall's earlier hit, the romantic fantasy *Pretty Woman*.

The only person to come out smelling like a rose, or like fresh leather, is Rosie O'Donnell, who with Dan Aykroyd as her partner plays a square undercover cop assigned to Club Eden, a sort of Silicone Valley of the Dolls. O'Donnell actually looks rather fetching in her dominatrix disguise.

"Tell me I look gorgeous from behind," she instructs her sex slave. It would not have been such a bad movie if by the end, O'Donnell and Delany had switched roles.

The movie's touted erotica is compromised by set design. Club Eden is envisioned as the Las Vegas of sex, so gaudy and kitschy it looks modeled on the beauty island of *In Like Flint*. Particularly unhelpful is the dime-store psychology as to why some people get hot and bothered when treated like slime. "All this ceremony and ritual makes me so aroused," offers one elderly clubgoer.

Mercurio was obviously cast on the strength of his buns after displaying them in tights as he tangoed to international reknown in the Australian dance satire *Strictly Ballroom*. He is tied to a post and suffers the indignity of Mistress Lisa administering a hairbrush spanking. Guess what? He likes it.

More embarrassing is when Hector Elizondo as the club's major domo explains it all to Mistress Lisa: "I am a top, a master, and you are a bottom, a submissive . . . Welcome to my world."

The ultraslim Delany's frequent full-frontal nude scenes are very easy on the eyes—especially after the downer of seeing her in *Light Sleeper*, where she plays a wretched drug addict who starts off "dripping" for her hot sex scenes with WILLEM DAFOE, but eventually takes a long walk off a short

Steve Martin lets his fingers do the walking toward Delany's breast in the comedy *Housesitter*.

. . . .

(Opposite) Hoping to change her girl-next-door image, Dana Delany in *Exit to Eden* plays the least terrifying dominatrix ever to crack a whip.

. . . .

FILMOGRAPHY

The Fan, 1981
Almost You, 1984
Where the River Runs Black, 1986
Moon Over Parador, 1988
Patty Hearst, 1988
Masquerade, 1988
Light Sleeper, 1992
Housesitter, 1992
Batman: Mask of the Phantasm
(voice), 1993
Tombstone, 1993
Exit to Eden, 1994
Live Nude Girls, 1995

window sill in her nightgown. *Exit to Eden* indulges only in the softest of soft-core antics, as if nude volleyball were the *ne plus ultra* in erotic fantasy.

Yet, for Delany, making this movie was an important career decision. "The nude scenes don't bother me and don't scare me," she says. "This is something I've always wanted to do because people tend to typecast me as the girl next door."

Rosie O'Donnell (with stiletto on submissive Dan Aykroyd) makes a more believable dominatrix in *Exit to Eden*.

Diane Keaton

It Ain't Over Till It's Over

MERYL STREEP becomes an action heroine. GOLDIE HAWN is still showing her butt. But as Diane Keaton nears fifty, the body is something to be swathed in enough layers to survive an Arctic winter.

"It's over," moaned Keaton in an interview after making *Manhattan Murder Mystery*, which reteamed her in 1993 with former flame and costar Woody Allen.

What's over? Her body—or so she says. Born in Los Angeles in 1946, the actress dissociates herself from others of her generation like Streep and Hawn to give up entirely on things sexual, even though physical comedy is one of her specialties.

Keaton has always been endearingly prudish, even though one of her early films, the sensationalist *Looking for Mr. Goodbar* (1977), gave her several topless scenes in her quest for the perfect one-night stand. She shows little ego about how she is filmed. "I'm not that kind of actress. If you worry about

Diane Keaton eyes Richard Gere for a one-night stand in *Looking for Mr. Goodbar,* the only movie in which she goes topless.

which is your good side, you're involved in a kind of acting that I'm not interested in. It takes away from the fun of it if what I'm thinking is, 'Oh, if I move three inches to the right and keep my chin up'. What's fun about the whole thing is what you're feeling, keeping it alive. That means you can't be thinking about how you look."

Her dithering indecision and comically bottomless insecurity were the basis for her character in the semiautobiographical *Annie Hall,* Woody Allen's 1977 recreation of his breakup with Keaton. With that movie, she won an Academy Award and started a fashion revolution. In the years since, while other women have gone on to slinky microwear, Keaton has stuck with the Annie Hall look that she created.

With her bangs flopping a protective curtain over eyes that turn down sweetly at the outer edges, Keaton projects an appeal based on a silly vulnerability. She's a funny little valentine that cerebral men—like Allen and later boyfriends WAR-REN BEATTY and Al Pacino—want to rescue and educate. She plays the kind of women who fight until they melt, as she does with country veterinarian Sam Shepard in *Baby Boom* in 1986, or with Pacino in the *Godfather* movies. In *Mrs. Soffel* (1984), as a repressed prison warden's wife, merely touching

Mr. Goodbar was the exception to the rule—usually Keaton goes to absurd lengths to cover herself in as many layers as possible.

Photo courtesy of Kevin Winter/DMI

FILMOGRAPHY

Lovers and Other Strangers, 1970
The Godfather, 1972
Play It Again, Sam, 1972
Sleeper, 1973
The Godfather, Part II, 1974
I Will ... I Will ... for Now, 1975
Love and Death, 1975
Harry and Walter Go to New York, 1976
Annie Hall, 1977
Looking for Mr. Goodbar, 1977
Interiors, 1978
Manhattan, 1979
Reds, 1981
Shoot the Moon, 1982
The Little Drummer Girl, 1984
Mrs. Soffel, 1984
Crimes of the Heart, 1986
Baby Boom, 1987
Heaven (documentary; filmmaker), 1987
Radio Days, 1987
The Good Mother, 1988
The Lemon Sisters, 1990
The Godfather, Part III, 1990
Father of the Bride, 1991
Manhattan Murder Mystery, 1993
Look Who's Talking Now (voice), 1993
Daddy's Little Dividend, 1995
Unstrung Heroes (director), 1995

prisoner MEL GIBSON's hand through the bars is enough to make her leave hubby and kids, orchestrate Gibson's prison break, and even die; so it's not as if she doesn't feel the passion. (She certainly does with LIAM NEESON in *The Good Mother*, 1988.)

In light of how modest she has been in her career—not just clothed, but clothed to the gills—it is almost embarrassing to see her naked in *Mr. Goodbar*, as if we had peeked through a keyhole. When she says "It's over," she seems to say it with as much relief as conviction, as if she no longer has to pretend to play the Hollywood game she never wanted to play in the first place.

k. d. lang

No Nautilus Machines Up North

For those who didn't get enough oomph from that *Vanity Fair* cover in which Cindy Crawford gave k. d. lang a close shave, there is *salmonberries*, lang's 1991 film debut. It rotted in the can for three years before finding a distributor.

salmonberries—artily lowercase, like its star's name—was concocted by writer/director Percy Adlon specifically for lang, and is notorious only for the singer's full-frontal nude scene.

It wasn't the first time that Adlon had filmed a leading lady in the altogether. In his German film *Sugarbaby*, ample actress Marianne Sagebrecht enjoyed several explicit scenes with a skinny train conductor. But lang came out nude in *salmonberries* before she had officially come out in the other sense of the phrase. By the time the movie was released briefly in 1994, her extensive lesbian following was primed to see her, then bitterly disappointed.

The movie is set in the freezescape of Kotzebue, a tiny Northwest Alaska town where lang (who herself grew up in Alberta) plays a pipeline worker named after the town itself. This Kotzebue is an odd duck of indiscriminate gender—she is passing as a he among the pipeline workers—who haunts the local library, presided over by a severe German émigré named Roswitha.

Madam Librarian is stern, remote, with upswept blond hair and a manner as frigid as the landscape. Kotzebue has an unrequited crush, and shows it the grade school way—by throwing books and tantrums.

Early in the movie, Kotzebue lets Roswitha in on the secret of her gender. She disappears for a moment in the back of the library, then returns to stand impassively naked in an aisle of books. It doesn't look as if there are too many Nautilus machines this far north, and an early screening for a predominantly lesbian audience was filled with hoots of derision. Fans

k. d. lang melts the icy local librarian in the frozen tundra setting of *salmonberries*, the singer's ill-advised naked film debut.

lang recovers from her embarrassing movie with a more
glamorous look, one that
requires clothing.

Photo courtesy of Alex Oliveira/DMI

FILMOGRAPHY

salmonberries, 1991
Even Cowgirls Get the Blues, 1993

can be so unforgiving.

"It was hard, especially when you don't have the body of KIM BASINGER," lang told the *San Francisco Chronicle.* "But then I thought—forget about that…I'm a big-boned gal. I'll just strip and present my body."

Those hoots of derision come in handy later in the movie as well. For instance, while lang's Grammy-winning voice on the soundtrack sings about walking through the snow barefoot, Roswitha actually takes off her shoes and socks and mushes on in subfreezing temperatures.

Another appropriate moment in which to hoot might be when lang attends a neighborhood bingo game—as jarring an image as you can get—or when she gets drunk on fermented berry preserves, or when she stands atop a barroom pinball machine to declare: "I am an Eskimo!" (One onlooker answers cryptically, "*We are all Eskimos.*")

Director Adlon's movies tend to favor oddballs stuck in out-of-the-way places, like the desolate roadside stop in *Bagdad Cafe.* Here, he puts two displaced persons in a place as displaced as you can get. The outcasts meet and nearly sleep together in the furthest outpost of society, a tundra of the human soul.

Although *salmonberries* had its day in the sun when it inexplicably won second prize at the Montreal Film Festival, it received a chilly reception when it opened in theaters—much like the reception granted another troubled movie in which lang sings, *Even Cowgirls Get the Blues,* based on the seventies Tom Robbins novel about oversized thumbs, freedom of movement, and lesbian cowgirls.

Based on these two movies, lang should stick to her day job.

Sean Young

"Sharon Stone's Body You Could Bounce Pebbles off, But Sean Is Vulnerable."

The only person to blame for Sean Young's excruciating nude scenes in *Love Crimes* is Young herself, who fought to have them reinstated in the "director's cut" video version.

The 1992 movie stars Young as a tenacious assistant district attorney on the trail of pervert Patrick Bergin. Posing as a *Playboy* photographer and talent scout, Bergin seduces women by playing on their vanity and their most hidden, forbidden sexual fantasies. "*Be* the horse! *Be* the horse!" he cries, whipping one woman on the rump as she snorts, rears, and makes like a mare in heat. After taking advantage of these women, he usually drives off with their cars as well.

Fighting her own sexual repression, Young goes undercover to ensnare Bergin. He quickly figures her out, locks her in a closet in his woodland cottage, then does lewd and lascivious things to her—which, it turns out, she kinda likes.

Taking on a character like this is not terribly unusual for the Kentucky-born, Ohio-raised Mary Sean Young, who by now has a reputation for doing wild and crazy things. A burgeoning sex bomb after the backseat limo scene with KEVIN COSTNER in *No Way Out*, Young later became known for two things, neither one really related to her acting talents. One was her shameless campaign to win the role of Catwoman in *Batman Returns*—she even wore a catsuit while pleading her case. The other was her ill-fated, off-screen affair with egomaniacal James Woods while making *The Boost*. That affair culminated in his never-proven charges that Young left a threatening voodoo doll on his fiancée's doorstep. (Wood's marriage ended not much later amid charges he had drawn a gun on his bride.)

So it was no surprise that Young might go out on a limb in *Love Crimes*, but her limbs turned out to be only part of the problem. She got heat for one scene in particular, where she stands up in the bathtub. The first problem with the scene is that it occurs at a point in the movie where the audience is wondering why her character doesn't use her spare time to flee her kidnapper instead of taking a bath. The second problem is that the nudity is unsettling. The scene is not as much about sexuality as vulnerability, and Young's body looks slim and fragile as a child's, not the way one would expect after that lubricious limo ride, or her brief toplessness in *The Boost* and *A Kiss Before Dying*.

"Sean knows she doesn't have one of those perfect L.A. silicone bodies," says Lizzie Borden, the feminist *Love Crimes* director who previously had made *Working Girls*, an almost documentary look at the daily grind of prostitution. "Her bravery and nervousness comes through. Not that many actresses will do full-frontal nudity in America, and Sean is both gutsy and insecure. She has a beautiful body, but it seems very very human to me. Sharon Stone's body you could

bounce pebbles off of, it's so impeccable, while Sean's vulnerability and even her almost adolescent awkwardness about her body works with the character, along with her own tendency to get skinny, almost anorexic at times. She's aware of her body's flaws but it's important for her to show herself."

The movie was chopped and reformed for its theatrical release, then reconstituted somewhat to its original shape for the video release by Borden. The new "director's cut" contains about nine extra minutes, including some sorely needed character development. A lot of that character development takes place in the altogether.

For instance, there is one scene where Young tears her clothes off around a campfire as she comes to terms with her sexual repression. She rants, raves, and tries to stab Bergin with a knife. "At the time we were filming, Sean was so angry about that stuff with James Woods that she wanted to act out her anger," says Borden. "I didn't know she was going to rip her blouse open like that. I guess in some ways she felt it had relevance to her in her own life. When that scene didn't make the final cut for the theatrical version, Sean felt that the whole emotional point of the film had been cut out."

In the campfire scene, says Borden, "she freaks out and reveals her sexual problems and allows herself sexual fantasies about the guy. This is where you begin to understand her rea-

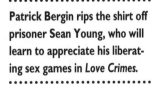

Patrick Bergin rips the shirt off prisoner Sean Young, who will learn to appreciate his liberating sex games in *Love Crimes*.

FILMOGRAPHY

Jane Austen in Manhattan, 1980
Stripes, 1981
Blade Runner, 1982
Young Doctors in Love, 1982
Baby ... Secret of the Lost
Legend, 1985
Arena Brains (short), 1987
The Boost, 1988
Cousins, 1989
Fire Birds, 1990
A Kiss Before Dying, 1991
Love Crimes, 1991
Hold Me, Thrill Me, Kiss Me, 1992
Fatal Instinct, 1993
Ace Ventura: Pet Detective, 1994

sons for going after this sex criminal, otherwise the movie doesn't make much sense. It's more perverse than overtly sexual. He spanks her and washes her. The sex criminal is being very tender to her, that's the perverse part of his character, because this was always meant as more of a psychological thriller than a straight thriller."

The attempt to make it a straight thriller came from a disastrous preview screening to impatient teenagers looking for a sexy action picture. Then came a battle with the MPAA's ratings board, which was discomfited by the context and frankness of the nudity. Trims were made to avoid the dreaded NC–17 rating.

"I wish no one would see the theatrical version, I wish it would disappear," says Borden. "I would have loved to make the movie even more explicit, and send it out as an art movie in twenty theaters. But there are ratings problems, that's one of the horrible things in this conservative environment. By initially cutting out scenes, Sean's character had no shape, and she was criticized for being very flat."

Young has the ability to make fun of herself, as she does with gusto playing killer babes in *Hold Me, Thrill Me, Kiss Me* (1992) and *Fatal Instinct* (1993). In *Ace Ventura: Pet Detective* (1994), she plays a sex-change virago whose kiss sends homophobic Jim Carrey into a comic frenzy of over-the-top disgust.

Striptease

STARS WHO WON'T GO ALL THE WAY, AT LEAST NOT OFTEN ENOUGH

Ann-Margret

How Lovely to Be a Woman

J ohn Wayne once said that if he were to die he wanted Ann-Margret to dance on his grave, because if anything could get him up, she could.

When Ann-Margret changes clothes during the "How Lovely to Be a Woman" number in *Bye Bye Birdie* (1963), the joke is that she ends up looking like a tomboy dressed in sweatshirt and baseball cap after trilling the virtues of her own mature femininity ("The wait was well worthwhile . . ."). But the real joke of the number's choreography is that the sexy actress—who later in the movie will promise to go so wild in her midriff blouse and capri pants that "daddy dear . . . you won't know your daughter!"—accomplishes this total wardrobe change without ever showing an indiscreet bit of flesh.

The original kitten with a whip has built a career on exuding sexuality. Director John Waters says one of the formative experiences of his youth was watching her throw a "glamour fit" in *Viva Las Vegas* (1964), the movie Ann-Margret made while getting as close off-screen to her costar, Elvis Presley, as

Ann-Margret's gotta lotta livin' to do, and Bobby Rydell is in the way, in *Bye Bye Birdie*, a movie in which she completely changes her clothes on-camera, without giving anything away.

FILMOGRAPHY

A Pocketful of Miracles, 1961
State Fair, 1962
The Pleasure Seekers, 1964
Viva Las Vegas, 1964
Bus Riley's Back in Town, 1965
The Cincinnati Kid, 1965
Once a Thief, 1965
Made in Paris, 1966
Murderers' Row, 1966
Stagecoach, 1966
The Swinger, 1966
Il Profeta, 1967
C.C. and Company, 1970
R.P.M., 1970
Carnal Knowledge, 1971
Un Homme est mort, 1973
The Train Robbers, 1973
Tommy, 1975
Folies bourgeoises, 1976
Joseph Andrews, 1976
The Last Remake of Beau Geste, 1977
The Cheap Detective, 1978
Magic, 1978
The Villain, 1979
Middle Age Crazy, 1980
I Ought to Be in Pictures, 1981
Lookin' to Get Out, 1982
The Return of the Soldier, 1982
Vice Squad, 1982
Twice in a Lifetime, 1985
52 Pick-Up, 1986
A Tiger's Tale, 1987
A New Life, 1988
Newsies, 1992
Grumpy Old Men, 1993

his gyrations would permit.

Audiences secretly (or maybe not so secretly) longed to see her take her clothes off. She did in a couple of 1970 movies. But when she did in *Carnal Knowledge* (1971), rolling about in bed and in the shower with Jack Nicholson, she was not only applauded, she was nominated for an Oscar.

The comedian George Burns, who had always joked about having an eye for the ladies, apparently wasn't kidding. He discovered singer-dancer Ann-Margret Olsson in a cabaret act and launched her career, which was full of harmless fluff until she played Nicholson's unhappy lover in Mike Nichols's *Carnal Knowledge*, a sharply observant dirge for sexual relationships.

Despite a seriously damaging fall off a stage ladder during rehearsals for a show in 1972, which required some reconstructive surgery, Ann-Margret's sex appeal has never diminished. She has occasionally done topless scenes (with and without a body double)—as in *Magic* (1978) and *A Tiger's Tale* (1988). In *Grumpy Old Men* (1993), her mere presence in the neighborhood causes a further rift between lifelong enemies and hormone victims Jack Lemmon and Walter Matthau. Just as in *Bye Bye Birdie*, she's always so tantalizing she leaves the impression that you've seen her disrobe even when it was done with smoke and mirrors and an artfully placed sweatshirt.

Alec Baldwin

Wheat Dreams

lec Baldwin was furious when a magazine interviewer relatively early in his career gushed about his hairy chest, calling it as lush as a field of wheat. Serious actors don't like their body parts described in excruciating detail. But sometimes serious actors become stars and get to command star salaries because their sexual charisma is what separates them from the pack.

This is what happened to Baldwin after a sturdy but unheralded career as a character actor. Everyone remembers MELANIE GRIFFITH's hilariously nean-derthal Staten Island boyfriend in *Working Girl* (1988), who assures her "it's not what it looks like" when she catches him fully flagrante delicto with one of her friends. And MICHELLE PFEIFFER's middle-class gangster husband who gets shot early on in *Married to the Mob* (1988). Baldwin was creating memo-rable roles, yet his name was not coming trippingly to the tongue.

Stardom and being a sex symbol came hand in hand (as it often does) in 1990 with *The Hunt for Red October*, in which Baldwin held his own against

the formidable Sean Connery aboard a Russian submarine. He lost the franchise on this Jack Ryan character in subsequent adaptations of Tom Clancy novels to Harrison Ford—either because stardom had gone to his head and he held out for too much money, or because he was expanding his artistic horizons by getting ready to do *A Streetcar Named Desire* on Broadway, depending on which reports you believe.

Baldwin radiates a supreme self-confidence, which in itself would be sexy even without the penetrating eyes, shock of dark hair, and aforementioned field of wheat. That intensity has been tapped in numerous movies, particularly *Glengarry Glen Ross* (1992), in which he plays the bastard from the front office who terrorizes his underlings at a motivational meeting. When asked his name, he spits: "*Fuck* you, that's my name."

Combining sexual heat with the icy aloofness that allows him to break a man's finger without breaking his stride in *Miami Blues* (1990), Baldwin plays a surgeon who makes arrogant decisions in the operating room in *Malice* (1993), a movie in which he healthily beds first his nurse and then downstairs neighbor NICOLE KIDMAN, who has lain awake nights listening to him go at it.

For a man who doesn't like his chest hairs examined, Baldwin shot some pretty hairy NC–17 rated scenes with bride KIM BASINGER in *The Getaway* (1994), a thieves-on-the-run remake that sank like a stone. The ardent love scenes look

A fake nose wasn't the only thing hiding parts of **Baldwin** in *The Shadow*. The actor had to be wrapped with a girdle because he wasn't "cut" enough for the bare-chested action scenes early in the movie.

FILMOGRAPHY

Forever, Lulu, 1987
Beetlejuice, 1988
Married to the Mob, 1988
She's Having a Baby, 1988
Talk Radio, 1988
Working Girl, 1988
Great Balls of Fire, 1989
Alice, 1990
The Hunt for Red October, 1990
Miami Blues, 1990
The Marrying Man, 1991
Prelude to a Kiss, 1992
Glengarry Glen Ross, 1992
Malice, 1993
The Shadow, 1994
The Getaway, 1994
Heaven's Prisoners, 1995
The Juror, 1996

impressively like the real thing—wasn't that the idea by teasingly casting the newlyweds?—although shot with artful amber shadows so that most of what we see is in silhouette.

Kelly Lynch, who costarred with William Baldwin in *Three of Hearts*, gets to try out another Baldwin brother when she plays Alec's wife in the torrid *Heaven's Prisoners* (1995), in which Alec is a recovering alcoholic sleuth down in the bayou.

Tom Cruise
Vampire's Kiss

So, what's under the bowl, Tom? Only Nicole knows, and she's not telling—although the look on her face has broad implications.

For an actor whose gorgeous looks were probably the motivating force behind his being cast by Dino DeLaurentiis in 1981's *Endless Love*, his first screen appearance, Tom Cruise has been enforcing much Cruise control over how his body is displayed. You have to be quick on your feet (or slow with your frame-by-frame advance) to notice his full-frontal shot in 1983's *All the Right Moves*. And the sight of his rear end is far from erotic in the context of the hospital scene in 1989's *Born on the Fourth of July*, when his character is adjusting to life after the Vietnam War as a paraplegic.

In other words, Cruise used his body and sex appeal to become a star, and now, he wants to be known as a bona fide actor.

Director Ron Howard had some fun with Cruise's aversion to screen nudity when he directed him in *Far and Away* (1992), in which Cruise plays a low-born Irish lad who makes good in the 1883 Oklahoma land rush. Cruise was cast alongside his wife, the Australian actress NICOLE KIDMAN, and we can only hope their real sex life is more rewarding than the chaste one we witness in *Far and Away*. There is a running gag that has each of them surreptitiously peeking at the other while undressing for bed; in this way, they get to check out each other's buns without making a commitment, while posing as sister and brother sharing a room in a Boston brothel.

Earlier in the movie, while they are still working out their class differences in Ireland, Cruise is recuperating in bed from a fight. He is completely exposed except for a bowl resting over a strategic part of his body. Kidman nurses him back to consciousness, but not before stealing a peek. Perhaps, this was an acting stretch for her—since as Cruise's wife she already knows what's under there—but her look of relieved surprise is such that you wonder why it takes the pair more than two hours of screen time to share their first kiss.

Thomas Cruise Mapother IV began life on July 3, 1962, in Syracuse, New York. After his unimpressive cameo in *Endless Love*, he showed a marked charisma in *Taps* (1981). After only a few movies, he hit pay dirt with *Risky Business* (1983).

It was a raging point of controversy when Cruise was cast as the soulless eighteenth-century French vampire Lestat in

Tom Cruise bends to suck in *Interview With the Vampire*, a homoerotic movie which finds him giving **Brad Pitt** a love bite so ecstatic they float on air.

Caption: Marrieds Cruise and Nicole Kidman in the surprisingly (and disappointingly) tame *Far and Away*, posing as brother and sister while they secretly check out each other's butts.

FILMOGRAPHY

Endless Love, 1981
Taps, 1981
All the Right Moves, 1983
Losin' It, 1983
The Outsiders, 1983
Risky Business, 1983
Legend, 1985
The Color of Money, 1986
Top Gun, 1986
Cocktail, 1988
Rain Man, 1988
Born on the Fourth of July, 1989
Days of Thunder, 1990
Far and Away, 1992
A Few Good Men, 1992
The Firm, 1993
Interview With the Vampire, 1994
Mission Impossible, 1995

the 1994 film version of Anne Rice's addictive novel *Interview With the Vampire*. Later, Rice recanted her own suspicions about Cruise in an unprecedented two-page ad in *Daily Variety* and the *New York Times* (paid for by producer David Geffen), but there are those who still think Daniel Day-Lewis or Jeremy Irons would have made a more appropriately decadent choice.

In *Interview*, the bloodsucker's life is a solitary, but very stylish one—a lonely, intermittently rewarding, hedonistically alternative lifestyle. It's a very sexy Boys' Night Out with hunks Cruise, Brad Pitt, Stephen Rea, and ANTONIO BANDERAS cruising each other across the millennia and sucking each other's ecstatically exposed necks. "I'll give you the choice I never had" is the pickup line used by Lestat as he stakes out tender young morsels—the choice being between death or immortality, the subtext being a choice between the ordinary dating life or a new kind of sexuality fraught with anonymous encounters, passionate gorging of desires, and dangerous exchanges of bodily fluids.

The movie is told in a series of flashbacks as the regretful vampire Pitt gives an interview to Christian Slater about how Lestat resurrected him from his existential misery in the eighteenth century by ravishing him, draining him, then granting him the vampire's kiss of immortality, an embrace so ecstatic they floated upwards like Superman and Lois.

Yet another satisfied customer who must have peeked under the bowl.

Jodie Foster

The Wild Child Goes Skinny-Dipping

U sually, actresses begin their careers naked and cover up in direct proportion to how high they climb the career ladder. With Jodie Foster, it's been the opposite.

The two-Oscar'd cool beauty—with her Yale pedigree, unflinching gaze, and chiseled features—has been acting since she was a child, born Alicia Christian Foster in Los Angeles on November 19, 1962. Yet she never succumbed to the usual Hollywood pressure of looks over talent. Unless you count brief glimpses in *The Accused* (1988) or *Backtrack* (1989)—or the fact that she was a Coppertone baby with her tan line exposed by a persistent dog—Foster has kept her skin to herself.

Which has been just as well, since Foster more than many actresses represents a cerebral sort of beauty, a powerful, fiercely intelligent, and independent woman who has made her own way in a crazy business while keeping her priorities and sense of humor. "She manages to make intelligence erotic,"

says Jonathan Demme, who directed Foster as the persistent FBI trainee Clarice Starling in *The Silence of the Lambs* (1991). "There might be something dry in a way about intelligence, but watching her use that mind of hers is very intoxicating."

"I try to play true characters. They don't all have to be brilliant law school graduates," says Foster. "What I try to do is play characters that have been sheltered from the mainstream."

So, although her sexy magazine covers show that Foster has spent as much time in a gym as in the French literature section of the library, no one expected her to suddenly drop her drawers.

Hitman Dennis Hopper falls prey to target Jodie Foster's charms—some of which are very nearly on display here—in *Backtrack*.

With the benefit of hindsight, perhaps we could have seen it coming. In succession, she played a prostitute in bed with (of all people) Woody Allen in *Shadows and Fog* (1992), a plantation wife who goes to bed with someone impersonating her long lost husband (RICHARD GERE) in *Sommersby* (1993), and a heaving-bosomed swindler in the Old West, who is MEL GIBSON's match, in *Maverick* (1994).

With all those bedroom scenes so recently under her belt, she threw caution and clothing to the wind in *Nell* (1994), in which she plays a wild child discovered in a forest primeval by LIAM NEESON and Natasha Richardson. "Nell and May, chicopay!" she sing-songs in her own special language as she plunges nekkid as a jaybird into the moonlit river each night. The frequent nudity is justified by the storyline, of course,

FILMOGRAPHY

Napoleon and Samantha, 1972
Kansas City Bomber, 1972
One Little Indian, 1973
Tom Sawyer, 1973
Alice Doesn't Live Here Anymore, 1974
Bugsy Malone, 1976
Echoes of a Summer, 1976
Freaky Friday, 1976
Taxi Driver, 1976
Candleshoe, 1977
Il Casotto, 1977
The Little Girl Who Lives Down the Lane, 1977
Moi, fleur bleu, 1977
Moves Are My Life, 1978
Carny, 1980
Foxes, 1980
O'Hara's Wife, 1982
The Hotel New Hampshire, 1984
The Blood of Others, 1984
Mesmerized, 1986
Five Corners, 1987
Siesta, 1987
The Accused, 1988
Stealing Home, 1988
Backtrack, 1990
Little Man Tate (also director), 1991
The Silence of the Lambs, 1991
Shadows and Fog, 1992
Sommersby, 1993
Maverick, 1994
Nell, 1994

since Foster doing a gratuitous nude scene would be too great a shock.

"Why is it that whenever we mention nudity, people always think of sexuality?" Foster said after making *Nell*, for which she was nominated for an Oscar. "Our bodies are what we use to walk around, to sing, but at the same time, yes, this is meant to be very sensuous."

Actually, some of the skinny-dipping scenes were done in a wetsuit, because Foster figured that once she did her dive into the water, no one could see beneath the surface anyway. The movie was filmed in Tennessee in April and May, and the water was still icy. KEVIN COSTNER used the same excuse for using a body double in the water scenes of *Robin Hood: Princes of Thieves.*

Neeson, who also has to get the social innocent to button up her shirt in public, spies upon Foster's bare swim from a distance. "I think she's beautiful," he rhapsodizes. With this, he speaks for the audience as well.

Liam Neeson

Cary Grant, in and out of Tux

Liam Neeson is a hunk. Current bride Natasha Richardson and former flames Barbra Streisand, BROOKE SHIELDS, Jennifer Grey, Helen Mirren, Sinead O'Connor, and JULIA ROBERTS couldn't all be wrong.

What gives him hunk status? It's the commanding six foot, four inch frame, the gentle eyes behind intellectual wire-rim glasses and flop of hair, the lilt from rural Ballymena, Ireland, the off-kilter nose that was broken in a boxing match at fifteen and never properly reset, and the weathered hands of a former truck driver and forklift operator. On top of that, he's a superb actor, at home on film or on stage, and equally at ease in a languid, reclining nude shot on the beach for *US* magazine, one knee artfully raised. The *New York Times* calls him "a Sequoia of sex" and tactfully points out that "watching him does not create stress in the audience."

When neurotic and newly separated Judy Davis is set up with him in *Husbands and Wives* (1992), she's impervious to his charms until Mia Farrow

FILMOGRAPHY

Excalibur, 1981
Krull, 1983
The Bounty, 1984
Duet for One, 1986
The Mission, 1986
A Prayer for the Dying, 1987
Suspect, 1987
The Dead Pool, 1988
The Good Mother, 1988
High Spirits, 1988
Satisfaction, 1988
Next of Kin, 1989
Darkman, 1990
Crossing the Line, 1991
Husbands and Wives, 1992
Leap of Faith, 1992
Shining Through, 1992
Under Suspicion, 1992
Deception, 1993
Ethan Frome, 1993
Schindler's List, 1993
Nell, 1994
Rob Roy, 1995
Before & After, 1995

(Preceding page) Ruggedly handsome Irish actor Liam Neeson (shown here in *Crossing the Line*) combines an intellectual look with the weathered hands of a former forklift operator.

explains that he's so sensitive he weeps. Davis does a double take, narrowing her eyes and peering at him with new interest. "He *weeps?*" she asks keenly.

"The stone-faced men who don't show any emotion, they're not true heroes anymore," Neeson has said. "There's a Cary Grant in me bursting to get out, who wants to put on a tuxedo and be romantic and dashing and yet fall over the chair on the way out the door."

He may want to put on the tux, but palpitating viewers are hoping the Oscar nominee (for *Schindler's List*, 1993) will take it off—as he did ever so briefly in *Duet for One* (1987) and *Under Suspicion* (1992).

In *Nell* (1994), he finally joins wild child JODIE FOSTER for a naked swim under the watchful eye of Richardson, who met and married Neeson after they did *Anna Christie* together on Broadway. In *Nell*, Foster has been raised to fear men, and Neeson's task in this scene is to gradually introduce her to the wonders of male anatomy. He strips and sits on a rock, at first covering himself with his hands and then nervously and self-consciously revealing all to the unfettered girl in the water.

She finds what she sees totally unthreatening, which is not what some of Neeson's ex-girlfriends have reported. But then, you have to consider that the movie was shot in April, and the water must have been very cold. "It was worse for Jodie," said Neeson. "She was, basically, freezing. But the nudity all felt very natural when we were filming it. I think some people were concerned that it might be interpreted in some other way—you know, with sexual overtones"—the way it is meant to be interpreted in the original stage play. "Jodie and I just tried to keep our moment of nakedness very simple and pure, and hopefully that purity comes across."

Nick Nolte

Too Hot for Barbra

Like many stars for whom their looks are inevitably part of their resumé, Nick Nolte has undergone several physical transformations during his career. A big, bearish man, whose shaggy, heavyset appearance was even puffier during a period of hard drinking, Nolte later slimmed down, spruced up, tucked and tightened a few things (he jokingly called it a "testicle tuck"), and completely changed his image.

Nolte was born in Omaha, Nebraska, on February 8, 1941. Whether shaggy or streamlined, Nolte has always exhibited an outsized sex appeal, starting with *Rich Man, Poor Man*, the television miniseries that catapulted him to fame. In *North Dallas Forty* (1979), he played an irreverent football jock, who we see climbing naked into the locker-room whirlpool bath. The next time he mooned the camera was under grungier circumstances, as a bum taken in like a pet by a rich family in *Down and Out in Beverly Hills* (1986), and later as a con who makes good in *Weeds* (1987).

Nolte's intensity is a big part of his allure, so that in *New York Stories* (1989), he is completely believable as a driven painter who needs constant female inspiration, particularly from Rosanna Arquette's well turned ankle.

In 1991, his beefy, callow days behind him, Nolte was unnaturally slim as the lawyer battling ex-con ROBERT DE NIRO in *Cape Fear.* He said he purposely lost so much weight to differentiate his character from that of De Niro, who had pumped up his body to look like a man who had nothing to do all those years in jail except lift weights.

Nolte has the same intensity in person that he has on-screen, yet he has remained relatively modest in his love scenes.

Not that he has anything against them. In fact, it was he who encouraged *Prince of Tides* costar and director Barbra Streisand to go for it. "When we were doing the love scenes at first, the love scenes would just get hot. Really hot," says Nolte. "Just when they would start to really work, Barbra would yell, 'Cut!' And I would say, Barbra, why are you cutting it, it's just getting good!"

Streisand eventually agreed with Nolte after watching the dailies, yet she cut a scene from the final version in which her breasts are exposed. Nolte attributes her shyness to the dynamics on the set; usually, an actress in a sex scene has a strong male director nearby who is watching out for her, to whom she can turn when she is uncertain. In Streisand's case, of course, she was both actress and director, so there was no one to turn to.

"Sometimes when an actor is doing a scene and it gets to that point of where it starts to happen real spontaneously, there's a tendency to want to jump out of the scene, and say, *whoa.* Every actor does that, not just Barbra Streisand," says Nolte.

He recalls his first meeting with Streisand. "I was doing *Q*

(Opposite) **Nick Nolte** in jungle form in *Farewell to the King*; the burly actor had dysentery during location shooting and lost enough weight that he appears haggard in some scenes.

FILMOGRAPHY

Return to Macon County, 1975
The Deep, 1977
Who'll Stop the Rain?, 1978
Heart Beat, 1979
North Dallas Forty, 1979
48 Hrs., 1982
Cannery Row, 1982
Under Fire, 1983
Teachers, 1984
Grace Quigley, 1985
Down and out in Beverly Hills, 1986
Extreme Prejudice, 1987
Weeds, 1987
Farewell to the King, 1989
New York Stories, 1989
Three Fugitives, 1989
Another 48 Hrs., 1990
Everybody Wins, 1990
Q & A, 1990
The Prince of Tides, 1991
Cape Fear, 1991
The Player, 1992
Lorenzo's Oil, 1992
I'll Do Anything, 1993
I Love Trouble, 1994
Mulholland Falls, 1995
Jefferson in Paris, 1995

& A at the time, and I think I weighed 230, and had a mustache out to *here* and black hair. I was playing a character who was scary to be around. And I was drinking red wine, and I remember she was very nervous I was going to spill wine on her white carpet."

Streisand recalls the meeting differently, saying she cast Nolte because of his eyes. "It was the combination of the pain I saw in his eyes, the complexity behind his eyes, and the pain I knew he had experienced in childhood, and his relationships with women," she says. "And I think he was also at a vulnerable place in his life, ready to explore feelings, and romantic feelings, and sexual feelings, and deep, secretive feelings. It was important that the character be very, very male, and then make this transformation and be willing to go through this catharsis."

It was a catharsis for Nolte just to talk about his feelings with Streisand in their after-hour rap sessions about the nature of love. "We get down to the basic fact of living with each other as human beings, it's more of a human love," he says. "I think that's the way we have our families, it's balanced out, but we still carry this mythology of romantic love, which is a concept that basically came out of the twelfth century."

Michelle Pfeiffer
A Little Goes a Long Way

In that formfitting leather catsuit and her whip at the ready in _Batman Returns_ (1992), Michelle Pfeiffer could have segued from mournful beauty to a career as a dominatrix. Instead, she immediately followed that role with _The Age of Innocence_ (1994) as a turn-of-the-century countess who sends Daniel Day-Lewis into a sweat every time she unbuttons a glove or fans herself.

A little skin goes a long way with the willowy Pfeiffer, who slithered across the top of a grand piano, entreating Jeff Bridges to make whoopee with her in _The Fabulous Baker Boys_ (1989), without once revealing more than her shapely spine.

In person, Pfeiffer is almost painfully thin and can be very shy; perhaps, it is this real-life diffidence that has kept her from doing nude scenes. Although alluring, she does not have the exhibitionistic tendencies that help certain actors get through the mortifying ordeal of shooting take after take of a nude scene, surrounded by cast, crew, and often the suits from the front office who visit the set for the thrill of it.

Although you can catch very brief glimpses of her body in *Into the Night* (1985), *Tequila Sunrise* (1988), and *Frankie & Johnny* (1991), Pfeiffer demonstrates how it is possible to always appear enticing without ever taking her clothes off.

A sleeping Pfeiffer brings out the beast in Jack Nicholson in *Wolf,* about a man undergoing a hairy midlife crisis.

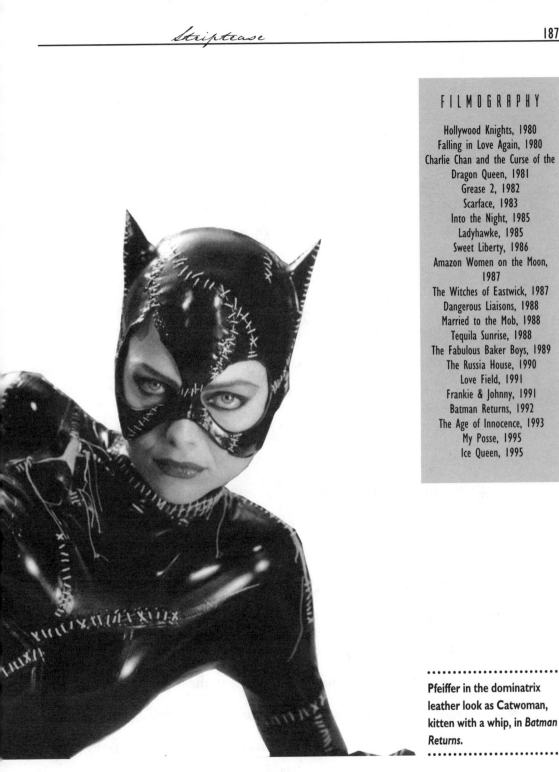

FILMOGRAPHY

Hollywood Knights, 1980
Falling in Love Again, 1980
Charlie Chan and the Curse of the
Dragon Queen, 1981
Grease 2, 1982
Scarface, 1983
Into the Night, 1985
Ladyhawke, 1985
Sweet Liberty, 1986
Amazon Women on the Moon,
1987
The Witches of Eastwick, 1987
Dangerous Liaisons, 1988
Married to the Mob, 1988
Tequila Sunrise, 1988
The Fabulous Baker Boys, 1989
The Russia House, 1990
Love Field, 1991
Frankie & Johnny, 1991
Batman Returns, 1992
The Age of Innocence, 1993
My Posse, 1995
Ice Queen, 1995

Pfeiffer in the dominatrix leather look as Catwoman, kitten with a whip, in *Batman Returns*.

Keanu Reeves

All Things to All People

For an actor as unconcerned with nudity in his personal life as the gossip columns allege, Keanu Reeves has certainly been keeping it all to himself on-screen.

Aside from a couple of brief bun shots in *My Own Private Idaho* (1991), where he plays a Shakespeare-spouting male hustler, and in *Point Break* (1991), where he plays an FBI agent pulled into the intoxicating adrenaline of surfing and skydiving, Reeves has been a Gen-X pinup since 1987 without having to doff more than a shirt.

There certainly have been suitable occasions for nudity in Reeves's movies. In 1988, he played UMA THURMAN's glandular eighteenth-century music teacher in *Dangerous Liaisons*. In *Bram Stoker's Dracula* (1992), Reeves plays a realtor trapped in Gary Oldman's castle and left to the orgiastic bloodsucking designs of some female creatures of the night. And in *Little Buddha* (1994), Reeves is photographed by director Bernardo Bertolucci as if he really is the

holy reincarnation of Prince Siddhartha. At least in *A Walk in the Clouds* (1995), he is scheduled to have sex in a vat of grapes; it's a start.

Reeves, whose Hawaiian first name means "cool breeze over the mountains," changed his early floppy-haired, laid-back Valley Boy image in 1994 with *Speed*, a successful attempt at the action genre. With a newly bulked-up body and buzz cut, Reeves went from his dumb *Bill & Ted* persona to the strong, silent type as he commandeers a bomb-rigged bus full of innocent passengers.

Raised in Canada, Reeves hated high school, flunked twelfth grade twice, and describes his younger self as being "an apathetic loner" and "the class clown." As he was turning thirty in 1995, he had yet to make good on an old promise that this would be the year he would "take deportment classes" so he could be the new "Cary Grant dude." However, he did hire a voice coach before appearing as the great Dane in a Winnipeg production of *Hamlet*.

Part of Reeves's success stems from his willingness to satisfy the fantasies of both male and female viewers. His campfire scene with fellow hustler River Phoenix in *Private Idaho* contained obvious homosexual overtones, and he was once quoted as telling someone: "I'm not heterosexual and I'm not homosexual, I'm just sexual."

FILMOGRAPHY

Youngblood, 1986
Flying, 1986
River's Edge, 1987
Dangerous Liaisons, 1988
The Night Before, 1988
Permanent Record, 1988
The Prince of Pennsylvania, 1988
Bill & Ted's Excellent Adventure, 1989
Parenthood, 1989
I Love You to Death, 1990
Tune in Tomorrow, 1990
My Own Private Idaho, 1991
Point Break, 1991
Bill & Ted's Bogus Journey, 1991
Bram Stoker's Dracula, 1992
Much Ado About Nothing, 1993
Freaked, 1993
Even Cowgirls Get the Blues, 1993
Little Buddha, 1993
Speed, 1994
A Walk in the Clouds, 1995
Speed 2, 1995
Feeling Minnesota, 1995

Keanu Reeves has managed to be a pinup boy without having to unpin much of his clothes; this may change now that *Speed* has put the emphasis on his brawn.

Julia Roberts

Throbbing Vein

Those lips, those legs.

Well, maybe just those lips. Julia Roberts's famously leggy opening scenes getting dressed in a micromini in the 1990 movie *Pretty Woman* featured the legs of Shelley Michelle, a professional body double. When even Roberts's legs don't pass muster, you know Hollywood standards are running way too high.

The incredibly brief nude scene with RICHARD GERE in that movie, shot through the headboard of a bed, features Roberts herself in the flesh; the *Bare Facts Video Guide* notes that it is indeed Julia because of her habit of getting a throbbing vein in her forehead "whenever her blood pressure goes up."

Although there are actresses with more range, Roberts has an incredible love affair with the camera. The wide-lipped smile, tawny reddish mane, belladonna-bright eyes, and trembly vulnerability have earned her two Oscar nominations (for *Steel Magnolias*, 1988, and for *Pretty Woman*), and the honorof being the biggest female box-office draw of the early nineties.

She's slim and gorgeous, yet every sex scene she has done has been coy in the extreme, from the artfully placed bubbles in her *Pretty Woman* bath to the terrycloth robes and under-the-sheets frolicking with Tim Robbins in *Ready to Wear* (1994). The romance implied by the John Grisham novel *The Pelican Brief* turned into a professional relationship between her and Denzel Washington in the 1993 movie version—undoubtedly because of the interracial element. And although she had the requisite sex promised by the title of *Sleeping With the Enemy* (1991), she showed little to abusive husband Patrick Bergin that she wouldn't show during an ordinary trip to the Laundromat.

That Roberts keeps herself under wraps is as elusive a mystery as her love life, in which she has stormily dated a succession of her leading men, including LIAM NEESON, Dylan McDermott, and Kiefer Sutherland. She married Lyle Lovett after they had both been in the *The Player*, but never in the same scene together; they split shortly thereafter.

"I was a rugged individualist at thirteen years old, and it worked out for me," says Roberts to describe her attitude toward life. "I learn a lot of personal stuff doing movies. I'm a lot stronger a person than I thought I was." And she never lets her slip show.

Endearing prostitute Julia Roberts does the cute chin-on-shoulder thing with aloof patron Richard Gere in *Pretty Woman*; those legs, slender and shapely though they are, were subbed by a body double in the movie's opening scenes.

FILMOGRAPHY

Blood Red, 1986
Satisfaction, 1988
Mystic Pizza, 1988
Steel Magnolias, 1989
Flatliners, 1990
Pretty Woman, 1990
Sleeping With the Enemy, 1991
Dying Young, 1991
Hook, 1991
The Player, 1992
The Pelican Brief, 1993
I Love Trouble, 1994
Prêt-a-Porter (Ready to Wear), 1994
Mary Reilly, 1995

Madeleine Stowe

Men Just Want to Protect Her

For all of doe-eyed Madeleine Stowe's sex appeal, she doesn't disrobe as often as she should. Maybe it's because it took her a while to get over the bad experience of making *China Moon*, a movie she has publicly regretted.

Double Indemnity was good for Barbara Stanwyck. *Body Heat* was good for KATHLEEN TURNER. But *China Moon*, another moody film noir in which a ravishing married lady twists a hapless guy around her little wedding-banded finger, did nothing to advance Stowe's career. Made in 1991 by Orion, but caught in the limbo of that studio's unfortunate bankruptcy, *China Moon* only surfaced in early 1994, way after *The Last of the Mohicans* and *Unlawful Entry* had made Stowe a classic figure of male desire.

The gorgeous Stowe, born in Eagle Rock, California, had shown bits and pieces of her anatomy from the time of her impressive film debut in *Stakeout*

....

Swooning Madeleine Stowe brings out the protective instincts of Daniel Day-Lewis in *The Last of the Mohicans*.

....

FILMOGRAPHY

Stakeout, 1987
Tropical Snow, 1989
Worth Winning, 1989
Revenge, 1990
The Two Jakes, 1990
China Moon, 1991 (released 1994)
Closet Land, 1991
The Last of the Mohicans, 1992
Unlawful Entry, 1992
Short Cuts, 1993
Blink, 1994
Bad Girls, 1994

(1987) as the object of Richard Dreyfuss's binoculars. She continued the trend with successively more impressive costars, such as KEVIN COSTNER in *Revenge* and Jack Nicholson in *The Two Jakes*. But although she looks wonderful in the moonlight of *China Moon*, taking a nighttime skinny-dip off a rowboat, Stowe would soon have the career clout to avoid such stilted and gratuitous scenes.

For instance, the nudity is brief but more necessary in *Unlawful Entry* (1992). In that movie, yuppie, ineffectual husband KURT RUSSELL is pitted against a blue-collar man in blue, psychotic cop Ray Liotta. Both men vie for Stowe in a testosterone contest over which one of them is better equipped to protect her. When the cop stumbles in upon her making love with her husband, it is fair to say that his breach of the integrity of their bedroom advances the plot and justifies the nudity.

While Daniel Day-Lewis's bare chest fills the screen in Panavision during the lushly romantic *Last of the Mohicans* (1992), Stowe manages to keep her bodice laced. Like *Unlawful Entry*, it's another rescue fantasy. This time, her wilderness-raised suitor risks waterfalls and slings and arrows to save Stowe from a savage tribe.

There must be something about Stowe's willowy strength that brings out the he-man rescuer among the menfolk, because detective Aidan Quinn does everything in his power to get her attention in *Blink* (1994)—he even wiggles his bare buns at her at a nightclub (to no avail since she is blind)—then comes to her aid when she is stalked by a killer.

And in the pseudofeminist (or soft-core porn, depending on how you look at it) *Bad Girls* (1994), Stowe is a tough-minded refugee from an Old West brothel who goes on the lam with DREW BARRYMORE, Mary Stuart Masterson, and Andie MacDowell—all of them wearing scanty lingerie on horseback. Was there no chafing in the Old West? Stowe is caught between a sadistic ex-boyfriend and the handsome varmint (Dermot

Mulroney) she meets on the trail who tenderly treats her wounds. We know Mulroney is a good guy because when he runs into her, she's totally nude except for her gun, yet he doesn't treat her disrespectfully or make a pass at her. The sight of Stowe's flesh brings out the tender side in men.

By 1993, Stowe must have gotten *China Moon* out of her system. This was the year she sat for a nude portrait for sister JULIANNE MOORE in Robert Altman's *Short Cuts*. Stowe's character's brother-in-law (Matthew Modine) walks in unexpectedly to see the two sisters conversing as if nothing were amiss, although Stowe is in her birthday suit with her head thrown back in a pose of ecstasy.

Later, Stowe gets off on tormenting her lying, cheating husband (Tim Robbins) about how game-show host Alex Trebek may be interested in buying the portrait. "You mean, like you were naked?" he asks.

"Nude, they call it," she replies evenly.

"You mean, without any underpants on, naked?"

"Mm-hmm."

Meryl Streep

From Accents to Lycra

An actress of Meryl Streep's stature would never have to undress like some ingenue starlet. So it must have been entirely her choice to flash a breast at KURT RUSSELL in *Silkwood* (1983) to further underscore her transition from a happy-go-lucky nuclear plant assembly-line worker who lives only for the pleasure of the moment to a politicized whistle-blower.

Even when Streep has played romantic roles, she has always carried such dramatic weight that she seems like the grande dame of acting. This is why she and ROBERT DE NIRO failed in *Falling in Love* (1984)—two such ferocious acting talents seemed declawed in this romantic trifle. And when she gazes out to sea for the lover who sailed away in *The French Lieutenant's Woman* (1981), it is hardly a lighthearted romp in the hay that comes to mind as Streep reaches deep into the gut to admit she was the French lieutenant's *whore.*

Streep, born Mary Louise Streep on June 22, 1949, in Summit, New

198

Meryl Streep (*right*) and
Goldie Hawn show what
becomes a legend most in
Death Becomes Her.

FILMOGRAPHY

Julia, 1977
The Deer Hunter, 1978
Kramer vs. Kramer, 1979
Manhattan, 1979
The Seduction of Joe Tynan, 1979
The French Lieutenant's Woman,
1981
Sophie's Choice, 1982
Still of the Night, 1982
Silkwood, 1983
Falling in Love, 1984
In Our Hands, 1984
Out of Africa, 1985
Plenty, 1985
Heartburn, 1986
Ironweed, 1987
A Cry in the Dark, 1988
She-Devil, 1989
Postcards From the Edge, 1990
Defending Your Life, 1991
Death Becomes Her, 1992
The House of the Spirits, 1993
The River Wild, 1994
Before and After, 1995
The Bridges of Madison County,
1995

(Preceding page) Lycra gave
Streep a career boost in *The
River Wild*, in which she has a
nude bathing scene watched
over by evil Kevin Bacon.

Jersey, is too deliberately intellectual to be thought of as a mere sex sym-

bol, and sex has never been part of her high-toned *oeuvre*. The brief nudity in *Still of the Night* (1982) and *A Cry in the Dark* (1988) is so unclear the movies may have employed body doubles. And her simulated oral sex scene with Ed Begley, Jr., in *She-Devil* (1989) went largely unnoticed since the movie was such a dud; Streep reportedly was furious over having been talked into making it.

So, it is interesting that at age forty-five, having always enjoyed respect but never a full command of the box office, Streep reconfigured herself into an action heroine with *The River Wild* (1994), as a former whitewater rafting guide who must steer her family through some dangerous waters under the watchful eyes of maniac Kevin Bacon. Streep practiced sculling for months just for the movie's opening shot of her powerfully rowing along the Charles. Streep seems to bask in the glow of her own newly acquired physical strength, as if to say that there's nothing any lithe, underclad bimbo can do on-screen that she can't do better.

And, of course, she's right.

Patrick Swayze

It's Like Butter

It doesn't seem fair that an actor with the body of both an athlete and a classically trained ballet dancer should be under lock and key as often as is Patrick Swayze. He was perfectly content to let his pelvis be the center of attention during *Dirty Dancing* (1987), and he will take off his shirt at the slightest plot provocation. But the only time you can catch him naked—and then only modestly from behind—is in *Roadhouse* (1989), in which he plays the best darn bouncer in the South.

If there's anything to hide on Swayze's body, it's probably his knees, which have sustained so many injuries from dancing, football, hockey, and roping cattle on his ranch that he could pose for the centerspread of a medical journal. He is so inured to pain that he once sliced off the tip of a finger with an electric planer and didn't notice until several hours later.

The Texas-born son of choreographer Patsy Swayze, Patrick studied ballet at the Harkness and Joffrey schools, danced with the Feld Company, and per-

Bar bouncer Patrick Swayze adopts a bare-chested kung-fu stance after Marshall Teague taunts him about prison conquests in *Road House.*

FILMOGRAPHY

Skatetown, U.S.A., 1979
The Outsiders, 1983
Uncommon Valor, 1983
Grandview, U.S.A., 1984
Red Dawn, 1984
Youngblood, 1986
Dirty Dancing, 1987
Steel Dawn, 1987
Tiger Warsaw, 1988
Next of Kin, 1989
Road House, 1989
Ghost, 1990
Point Break, 1991
City of Joy, 1992
Father Hood, 1993
To Wong Foo, Thanks for
Everything, Julie Newmar, 1995
Tall Tales, 1995
Three Wishes, 1995

formed in ice shows before becoming an actor. "I never wanted to be known as the Dance Dude," he says. "In the beginning of my career, I kept it quiet in order to fight the stigma of the dancer turned actor."

With such a background, he has excelled in physical roles, the most famous being the time he played a Catskills mambo instructor to a receptive Jennifer Grey in 1987 in *Dirty Dancing.* "The mambo is like a heartbeat," says Swayze as he demonstrates a few heart-stopping steps, fresh from a shower and clad only in black drawstring pants. "It's not an easy thing to get right. The feeling in mambo is that it has to feel like butter, loose, but with tension. That's the sexual aspect of this partner dancing—reserved dancing."

Perhaps, that's the key to what Swayze feels is sexy—keeping something in reserve. Although he and Kelly Lynch run naked into a pond at the end of *Roadhouse*—"Everything was bouncing, unfortunately" is how Lynch described the two of them—the most intimate thing about that movie is when a bruiser beating Swayze to a pulp puts him in a headlock and promises, "I used to fuck guys like you in prison!"

Now, everyone would like a taste of Swayze, a desire he fuels by wearing a corset and dress in *To Wong Foo, Thanks for Everything, Julie Newmar* (1995). "All I know is that I didn't have women screaming for me when I was growing up," he says. "It's a trade-off, being a star. Your privacy is gone. But then there's your career, so you deal with it. You deal with the fact that the way you zip up your zipper in the bathroom could wind up in the newspapers."

Art House Nudity

FOREIGN FILM BUFFS

Abril gets a leg up in *High Heels*, the Spanish sex comedy-melodrama in which she promised to do for parallel bars what *Tie Me Up* did for bubble baths.

Victoria Abril

Get Out Your Handkerchiefs

When that young turk of the Madrid cinema Pedro Almodóvar had a falling-out with his longtime muse Carmen Maura, he began substituting a younger actress, Victoria Abril. Her first film with Almodóvar was *Tie Me Up! Tie Me Down!*, where Abril was cast as a former porn star who is kidnapped by obsessed mental patient ANTONIO BANDERAS, tied to a bedpost, and forced to submit. Like all of Almodóvar's work, it's a comedy.

The director's signature is cheerful sexual perversion combined with high-camp melodrama. It's not just that Abril submits to her kidnapper, it's that she does so willingly, then falls in love with him.

Naturally, the MPAA had a fit. They branded the movie with an X, allegedly objecting to the harmless and funny scene in which Abril, naked in the bathtub, is playing with a toy frogman. She sends the toy snorkling down between her legs. (In *Sliver*, SHARON STONE masturbates in the bathtub sans frogman, and the slick studio-made movie got an R—but then, she kept her

FILMOGRAPHY

Cambio de Sexo (also song), 1976
Robin and Marian, 1976
Dona Perfecta, 1977
El Puente, 1977
La Muchacha de las Bragas de
Oro, 1980
Comin' at Ya, 1981
Asesinato en el Comite Central,
1982
J'ai epousé une ombre, 1982
Le Batard, 1983
Las Bicicletas Son para el Verano,
1983
La Colmena, 1983
The Moon in the Gutter, 1983
L'Addition, 1984
La Noche Mas Hermosa, 1984
Rio Abajo, 1984
Le Voyage, 1984
Tiempo de Silencio, 1985
After Darkness, 1985
La Hora Bruja, 1985
Rouge Gorge, 1985
Padre Nuestro, 1985
Max mon amour, 1986
Ternosecco, 1986
El Juego Mas Divertido, 1987
El Lute I, 1987
Baton Rouge, 1988
Ada dans la Jungle, 1988
Sans peur et sans reproche, 1988
Si Te Dicen Que Cai, 1989
A Solas Congito, 1990
Sandino, 1990
Tie Me Up! Tie Me Down!, 1990
High Heels, 1991
Lovers, 1992
Une Epoque formidable, 1991
Demasiado Corazon, 1992
Intruder, 1993
Jimmy Hollywood, 1994
Kika, 1994
Blue Helmet, 1994

pubic hair submerged.)

Almodóvar and his American distributor, Miramax, disputed the rating and finally released it without one. This is one of those arguments that the MPAA uses to ward off charges of censorship—that any movie can be released intact as long as it doesn't carry a rating. Practically speaking, though, an unrated movie's fate is a sad one—newspapers won't take ads for it, the public is suspicious or unaware of the movie's existence, and many theaters won't play it.

Ironically, *Tie Me Up!* is much tamer than much of Almodóvar's other work, so it particularly rankled the director that it didn't pass inspection. "I know that the lovemaking scenes in my movies are very realistic," says the director. "When you are telling a story, everything has to seem real, even science fiction has to have a reality. All my lovemaking scenes are in closeup, but you don't see anything, sometimes a breast. It's a kind of pity that when violence and sex are related with reality, the human reality, then you have a problem here. In American movies, there is no problem with *Total Recall*, because you don't recognize yourself in there, but when you're talking about reality, it's more problematic. In my movies, I try to be the most honest and sincere, in my way. I know sometimes it's a weird way, but that's my point of view, my mentality, and that's the reason to make a movie, to find expression."

One reason for Abril's success in collaborating with the demanding Almodóvar is that she is able to convey the particular Spanish sensibility that he likes in his leading ladies. No matter how outrageous the sexual situation, she approaches it with aplomb. Her attitude seems to be—expect the unexpected. This is why kidnapping, rape, and brutality have a strangely benign resonance in *Tie Me Up!*, something that would be very difficult to duplicate in an American movie, where actors are required to register appropriate moral indignation to relieve the audience's tension.

Abril, a single mother of two, was born in Madrid in 1960. She studied ballet as a teenager and only tried acting in order to finance her dance lessons. Her fluency in French and Italian quickly made her a European star way before she continued her Almodóvar connection with *High Heels* (1991), a film about the relationship between an actress mom and her newscaster daughter. Abril plays the daughter. "All I can say is that what we do for parallel bars is far more sexy than what I did in the bathtub in *Tie Me Up! Tie Me Down!,*" announced Abril.

What she did on the parallel bars was to hang from the rafters backstage at a drag show while an admirer ravages her.

Abril was even more provocative in *Lovers* (1992), based on a true-crime story, in which she is the older woman who indoctrinates her naive young tenant by stuffing a silk handkerchief up his bum and pulling it out during climax.

"Liberated roles are just not written here," she told *New York Daily News* columnist Robert Dominguez. "America is a democracy, but it is not tolerant in respect to sex—yet it *is* toward guns and violence."

Victoria Abril shows the form that makes Antonio Banderas want to tie her up, tie her down, and force her to become the mother of his children. The censors objected to her bathtub scene with an accommodating toy frogman.

Isabelle Adjani

Unmasked

Because Isabelle Adjani was so early identified with tragic romantic suffering in Trauffaut's masterful *The Story of Adèle H.* (1975), her striking looks—erotic pout, eyes flashing from a pale face—often bring to mind elaborate, secret madness, an inner romantic anguish of epic proportions.

In *La Reine Margot* (*Queen Margot,* 1994), she plays a man-hungry, unhappily married sixteenth century French royal. Her illicit love for Vincent Perez—he's the wrong class, the wrong religion, and the wrong politics, and anyway she's already married—takes on the burden of myth when she carts his severed head lovingly from the guillotine.

Audiences laugh inadvertently when she checks out the sweaty workmen along the waterfront disguised only with a flimsy mask around her eyes like the Lone Ranger. Who wouldn't recognize the gorgeous French actress, with or without mask?

Like many a European actress, Adjani has shown a lot of skin over the years. But now, as the reigning diva of French cinema (and the bearer of Daniel Day-Lewis's love child), she has the option of using body doubles—and she does liberally in the sumptuously photographed *La Reine Margot*, which premiered in a longer, bloodier version at Cannes than was later released in U.S. theaters.

Born in Germany of mixed German–Algerian parentage on June 27, 1955, Adjani made her film debut at fourteen and was already a star at age seventeen in the Comédie Française. She was nominated for her first Oscar for playing the obsessed daughter of Victor Hugo in *Adèle H.* Her second nomination was for *Camille Claudel* in 1988 as another obsessional, a sculptor in love with and abandoned by GERARD DEPARDIEU's Auguste Rodin. The director Jim Jarmusch pleaded with critic Joe Leydon to be allowed to accompany him to his Adjani interview after *Camille Claudel*, offering to hold the tape recorder just for the honor of being in the actress's presence.

While Adjani seems phosphorescent in *Margot*, she is eclipsed in that movie by the brief but satisfying unsheathing of costar Perez's manhood. Perez had previously played the mutual lover of Catherine Deneuve and her daughter in *Indochine* (1992), reportedly having two off-set affairs during filming, and the suitor in *Cyrano de Bergerac* (1990), who enlisted Depardieu to compose his love letters. He may not have had a rapier wit, but after *La Reine Margot*, one can see it

One of France's major exports, Isabelle Adjani projects sexuality with a touch of madness.

....

"I need a man!" growls Adjani in *Queen Margot*, and she finds more than enough of one in Vincent Perez, whose full-frontal scene upstages her.

....

FILMOGRAPHY

Le petit Bougnat, 1969
Faustine et le bel été, 1971
La Gifle, 1974
The Story of Adèle H., 1975
Barocco, 1976
The Tenant, 1976
Violette det François, 1977
The Driver, 1978
Nosferatu the Vampyre, 1978
Les Soeurs Brontë, 1978
Possession, 1981
Quartet, 1981
Tout feu, tout flamme, 1981
Antonieta, 1982
One Deadly Summer, 1982
Mortelle Randonnée, 1982
Subway, 1985
Ishtar, 1987
Camille Claudel (also coproducer), 1988
Lung Ta: Les cavaliers du vent, 1990
Toxic Affair, 1993
La Reine Margot, 1994

is possible that the sword is mightier than the pen.

A curious aside about the use or misuse of Adjani's physical attributes in cinema—she was seeing costar Warren Beatty while making *Ishtar*, and although she has one scene where she flashes a breast at Dustin Hoffman, during most of the movie, she is swathed head to toe in *chador*, the traditional Arab garment that covers all but a woman's eyes. Whatever Beatty was seeing off-screen, he was keeping it to himself.

Antonio Banderas

Baring the Neck, and More

For MADONNA, Antonio Banderas was the one who got away. Perhaps the only one.

One of the most embarrassing moments in her documentary *Truth or Dare* (1991) is when Madonna works hard to come up with the name of a man she hasn't yet had, decides on the hunky Spanish actor, then arranges to be seated next to him at a dinner party for maximum flirting purposes. She winds up leaving solo. Banderas later told reporters he wouldn't trade in his marriage and reputation for one night of sex with anyone, not even Madonna.

She had probably been smitten with his kinky sex scenes with VICTORIA ABRIL in *Tie Me Up! Tie Me Down!* (1990), where Banderas is a lunatic fresh from the asylum who decides that the way to find a wife is to kidnap former porn star Abril and tie her up, tie her down. (His method works, by the way.)

When Banderas shows flesh, his appeal is obvious. He has a *niceness* about

Gentle, devoted kidnapper and rapist Antonio Banderas eyes his prey, Victoria Abril, in *Tie Me Up! Tie Me Down!*

him, a soulfulness, a politeness that meshes perfectly with his soft good looks and smoldering gaze to give him the kind of erotic vulnerability female audiences crave in a romantic hero. No wonder Abril falls for him; such a sweet-natured kidnapper, such a polite rapist. She is touched by how he suffers a beating while trying to score drugs for her. Even his courtly rejection of Madonna at that party helps lend the actor an aura of someone who does the right thing.

The danger is that boyishness is a trait that doesn't age well. Fortunately, Banderas is not just a nice boy—he's a seething sensualist. Watch Bard Pitt go weak in the knees when he meets Banderas in *Interview With the Vampire* (1994).

Banderas was born in Málaga, Spain, in 1960. He studied music and drama and did theater in Madrid before his feature film debut in the bizarre sex comedy *Labyrinth of Passion* (1982), becoming one of the many Spanish stars introduced to Americans through the sex-saturated films of director Pedro Almodóvar.

Banderas made his U.S. film debut in *The Mambo Kings* (1992) as the more sensitive (naturally!) of two Cuban musician brothers (the other is Armand Assante), who try to make it big in the clubs and boudoirs of fifties New York. Madonna may have wanted him for his body, but he shows his facility for comedy in a scene in which he is sick with nerves over being a guest of fellow Cuban Desi Arnaz on *I Love Lucy*.

Banderas has what the song might call a fine romance with no kisses in Jonathan Demme's *Philadelphia* (1993), the first mainstream Hollywood picture to deal candidly with gays and AIDS. Banderas is the dying Tom Hanks's lover, although the movie is so chaste that they only share one kiss. "I thought to myself, Oh, my God, how disgusting," Banderas told *Movieline* about kissing a man previously in *Law of Desire* (1987). Ultimately, he found it "so easy. I didn't lose my fingers, my ear didn't fall down."

His casting in *Philadelphia* made sense in that he has the looks of a gay icon and the courtliness that assuages a possibly uptight mainstream audience. In any case, when Tom Hanks accepted his Oscar he thanked Banderas as the only man on the planet for whom he could leave his wife.

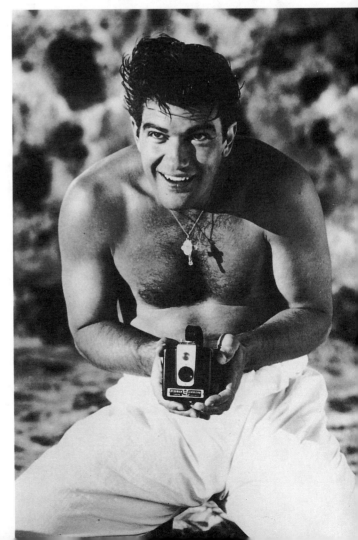

The torso that launched Banderas to international hunk status.

After a bleak stop as a romantic revolutionary who beds Winona Ryder in *The House of the Spirits* (1994), Banderas was back in the kind of form Madonna would appreciate in *Interview With the Vampire* (1994) as Armand, the sexiest and most charismatic of a cellar full of gorgeous bloodsuckers, including TOM CRUISE, Brad Pitt, and Stephen Rea. Armand, who always has a boy slave available for his friends to suck on, demonstrates his allure in a decadent theater piece, of which its climax has him seducing a nude woman and then turning her over to his followers for ravishment. His ultimate goal is to

FILMOGRAPHY

Labyrinth of Passion, 1982
Pestanas postizas, 1982
Y del seguro ... Libranos Señor!,
     1982
El señor Galindez, 1983
El caso Almeria, 1984
Los Zancos, 1984
Casa cerrado, 1985
La corte de Faraon, 1985
Requiem por un campesino
     español, 1985
27 horas, 1986
Matador, 1986
Puzzle, 1986
Asi Como Habian Sido, 1987
El Placer de Matar, 1987
Law of Desire, 1987
Baton Rouge, 1988
Mujeres al Borde de un Ataque de
     Nervios, 1988
Si Te Dicen Que Cai, 1989
Contra el Viento, 1990
Tie Me Up! Tie Me Down!, 1990
La Blanca Paloma, 1991
Cuentos de Borges I, 1991
Terra Nova, 1991
Truth or Dare (documentary), 1991
Bajarse al Moro, 1992
The Mambo Kings, 1992
Una Mujer Bajo la Lluvia, 1992
The House of the Spirits, 1993
Philadelphia, 1993
Shoot!, 1993
Interview With the Vampire, 1994
Of Love and Shadows, 1994
El Mariachi 2, 1995
Miami Rhapsody, 1995
Four Rooms, 1995

have the neck and then the company of Brad Pitt for the rest of eternity, an aspiration much of the audience might share.

This was not the actor's first brush with vampirism. Originally, Francis Coppola was so anxious to cast him as the lead in his *Bram Stoker's Dracula* (1992) that he had him read for the part in an empty church on Hollywood Boulevard. Banderas told *Movieline* that Coppola asked him to pretend he had a horrible secret, "Like, say, you killed your mother with a knife and hid her in a suitcase." In an Almodóvar film, of course, that would pass for comedy. In any case, Gary Oldman got the role and Banderas had to wait for his next *Interview*.

Juliette Binoche
"Nudity in the Eyes"

With her hair slicked back like an adolescent boy, Juliette Binoche is the ultimate nineties sex symbol—womanly yet boyish, tempting yet removed. This is what Lancôme is gambling on by hiring her to replace ISABELLA ROSSELLINI in 1996 as the face in their makeup ads. All Binoche needs now is a mainstream movie hit to propel her into the front ranks.

Damage (1992) could have been that movie, had it not sputtered and died. The French actress plays a femme fatale who proves very fatale indeed, causing a British politician's sexual, social, and moral downfall in R and NC–17 versions.

Her Anna Barton is to marry Rupert Graves, but she indulges in an obsessional affair with his father, JEREMY IRONS. Their torrid, nearly wordless *Last Tango*–style coupling is sweaty yet curiously cold. During the first visit by Irons, a pillar of British Parliament, Anna merely sits on her bed, then slides down the edge with her arms limply open to him. He takes her as it pleas-

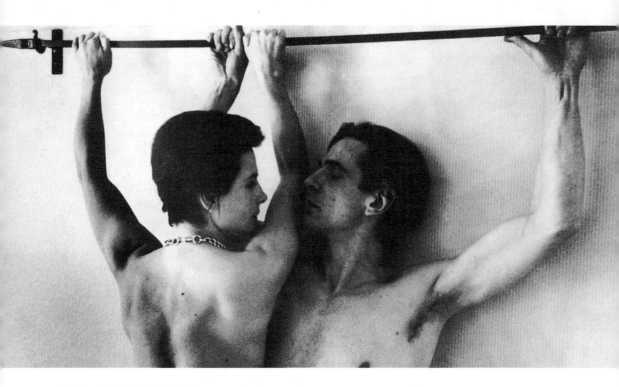

es him, which includes the kind of exertion that normally precedes a slipped disc.

The movie flopped despite its erotic material and a star of Irons's caliber. Audiences were puzzled by Binoche's character, repelled by the Oedipal triangle, and turned off by the sex itself. Irons hadn't wanted Binoche in the movie, and Binoche hated the brutal way Irons handled the love scenes.

Writer Josephine Hart, whose bestseller was the basis for the movie, took Irons's side, decreeing that his "intensity and despair and wildness were very disturbing to Juliette, but he was right. He is a drowning man, and he wants to be unified with her. It has nothing to do with lust, with a drive toward pleasure. Erotic obsession is a drive toward unity."

Oddly enough, the sex depicted here—rapacious, compulsive, stripped of the usual social meanings—is exactly why the movie works. When a man is secretly screwing his son's fiancée, there is no realistically happy outcome (unless we are in a French farce). The sex is meant to be disturbing.

As Binoche plays her, Anna is completely passive (more

accurate, passive-aggressive), lending her body totally to the statesman's unquenchable need, feeding his habit. Although the character is underwritten, Anna understands the man's obsession and the role she plays in it. When he tries to break things off, she knows this will break him as well, so she sends him a key to a new trysting spot where they can continue their affair more safely. She is not doing this only for his sake; Anna gets off on being that obscure object of desire.

It is the way in which Binoche transmits that Anna, though available, is unknowable that feeds the flames of the obsession. Although passion and obsession intersect at many points, passion is sweet and romantic despite the occasional destructive consequence, while obsession is dark and neurotic and is engineered to combust. Passion is easier on the tactile senses; obsession pricks at the nerve centers—a feeling that much of the pleasure-seeking movie audience hates. (Most people simply want to be entertained.) The sexy ad campaign for *Damage*—a poster of Irons leaning into Binoche with her hands above her head in a gesture of submission—primed the audience for a passionate sex romp, hence the disappointment.

A more important career step for Binoche was *Blue* (1993), the first of Polish director Krzysztof Kieslowski's trilogy inspired by the symbolic meanings of the French flag. Binoche was showered with awards for her portrayal of a woman suddenly liberated from her old life when her husband and child die in

Binoche works her way down Daniel Day-Lewis's chest in *The Unbearable Lightness of Being*.

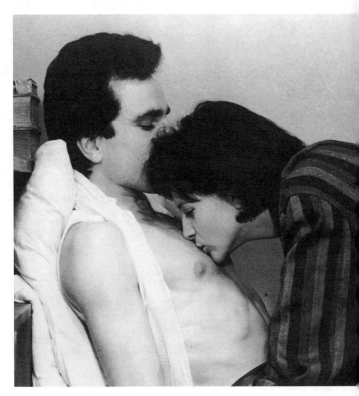

FILMOGRAPHY

Liberty Belle, 1983
Les Nanas, 1984
La Vie de famille, 1984
Je vous salue, Marie, 1985
Mon beau-frère a tué ma soeur, 1985
Rendezvous, 1985
Bad Blood, 1986
The Unbearable Lightness of Being, 1988
Un Tour de ménage, 1988
Les Amants du Pont Neuf, 1991
Damage, 1992
Emily Brontë's Wuthering Heights, 1992
Blue, 1993
White, 1994
Red, 1994

the movie's opening car wreck. Her recovery includes rewarding an old admirer with the sex that he craves (but not with the commitment).

American audiences, however, are more prone to think of Binoche from playing the prim wife of womanizer Daniel Day-Lewis in *The Unbearable Lightness of Being* (1988). This is the dual career she has had in the United States—thought of here mostly for her contribution to notoriously explicit movies, yet appreciated in Europe and by the art house crowd for her other work, including Jean-Luc Godard's *Hail, Mary* (1985).

Her eyes—despite rolling whitely up into her head as a blind girl in *Les Amants du Pont Neuf* (1991)—are her most potent feature, something that has not escaped Lancôme's attention. Most of the nudity in *Damage* belongs to Irons, a symbolic gesture of his undoing. But under Louis Malle's direction, Binoche's clear, unwavering gaze comes to signify the most explicit of come-ons, naughty, tantalizing, dangerous.

"Someone once asked if I felt like doing an action movie because I don't seem to move very much in films. I answered him, 'I breathe, I walk,'" Binoche has said. "The work that Krzysztof and I did together was like finding nudity in the eyes. My expression had to be clean and simple. Kieslowski told me, 'What I want to show is intimacy, your intimacy. I'm not interested in costumes.'"

Gerard Depardieu
The Starving Coal Miner Who Can't Quite Fit in the Tub

T he joke goes that all French movies are contractually obligated to star Gerard Depardieu, the country's chief commodity the way other countries depend on, say, the coffee crop.

Depardieu is certainly the best-known French actor of his time, a voracious and versatile performer who seems unafraid to tackle any subject matter. He's a wounded romantic with a nose for poetry in *Cyrano de Bergerac* (1990), a Christopher Columbus with a heavy French accent in *1492: The Conquest of Paradise* (1992), an unregenerate thug in *Going Places* (1974).

From that point of view, it makes sense that he would play Maheux, the patriarch of a poor coal-mining family in turn-of-the-century rural France in the epic *Germinal*, based on the hefty Emile Zola tome. He and wife Miou-Miou and what seems like their eighty-two-odd children put up a visitor who turns out to be an outside agitator trying to form a union.

The resulting strike throws everyone out of work, making them slowly

starve to death. There are lengthy, teary scenes of Miou-Miou serving her family the thinnest soup for dinner as the baby squalls.

The trouble with this casting is that Depardieu, a bon vivant who owns his own wine label, was physically enormous at the time he made this movie. No starving coal miner he.

Just when you think you can suspend disbelief, Maheux takes a naked bath in a barrel-like tub in the middle of the kitchen. Actually, he takes two naked baths, the first of which he follows up with a little slap-and-tickle with his wife; starving coal miners are still human, after all. But the sight of Depardieu's corpulence caused titters and then hilarity at the movie's U.S. premiere at the Sarasota French Film Festival. Unlike, say, Dennis Quaid, who lost forty pounds to look cadaverous as Doc Holliday in *Wyatt Earp*, Depardieu obviously did not prepare for his role by eating thin soup.

Of course, it is part of the movie's Frenchness that amid scenes of squalor and despair there is always time for a little full-frontal nudity. The painfully tiny Judith Henry plays Maheux's eldest daughter, who is so overheated pushing coal carts in the unventilated mines that she often works shirtless (naturally, the family is too poor to afford a bra).

Europeans are notoriously easier about the body, which is why you can see Depardieu sans coal dust many times in his career, all the way back to his first pairing with Miou-Miou in *Going Places*. Then, he was a slender, lithe thing, like his newly turned actor son Guillaume (*Tous les matins du monde*, 1992).

Depardieu enjoyed a peripatetic youth as a grade school dropout, juvenile delinquent, car thief, black marketeer, and even a towel boy at Cannes. He has carried that air of flaunting convention into his film career. You get the impression he would try any role, any position.

In fact, he was only sorry audiences didn't get to "see *all* of me"—meaning he was not erect—for an explicit sequence in *1900*; see the ROBERT DE NIRO entry for more details. Luckily, we didn't see all of him for the part in *The Last Woman* (1976), where he takes an electric carving knife to his privates. But we do see way, way too much of him as he strips naked in the existential police station in *A Pure Formality* (1994).

In *Ménage* (1986), he plays a tough yet tender burglar who falls in love with a henpecked husband. "It's a feminine work because it deals with seduction," said Depardieu over drinks during a visit to New York. "There is always the ambiguity of homosexuality in every man. It is more easy to show *la douceur*, softness, if you are an actor. Actors are very feminine."

As he speaks, partly in French and partly in his willy-nilly English, he gets excited, repeating key words, speaking faster, completely animated, hair flopping in his eyes. "It is harder to

FILMOGRAPHY

Cri du cormoran le soir au-dessus, 1971
Le Tueur, 1971
Un Peu de soleil dans l'eau froide, 1971
Le Viager, 1972
La Scoumoune, 1972
L' Affaire Dominici, 1972
Au Rendez-vous de la mort joyeuse, 1972
Nathalie Granger, 1972
Deux hommes dans la ville, 1973
The Holes, 1973
Rude journée pour la reine, 1973
Going Places, 1974
Stavisky, 1974
That Wonderful Crook, 1974
Vincent, François, Paul ... et les autres, 1974
Woman of the Ganges, 1974
Je t'aime, moi non plus, 1975
Mistress, 1975
Seven Deaths by Prescription, 1975
1900, 1976
Barocco, 1976
The Last Woman, 1976
La Nuit tous les chats sont gris, 1976
René la Canne, 1976
Violanta, 1976
Baxter, Vera Baxter, 1977
Dites-lui que je l'aime, 1977
Get Out Your Handkerchiefs, 1977
Die Linkshändige Frau, 1977
The Truck, 1977
Bye Bye Monkey, 1978
Les Chiens, 1978
Le Sucre, 1978
Cold Cuts, 1979
Le grand Embouteillage, 1979
Hurricane Rosy, 1979
Loulou, 1979
Mon Oncle d'Amérique, 1979

I Love You, 1980
Inspecteur la Bavure, 1980
The Last Metro, 1980
The Choice of Weapons, 1981
The Woman Next Door, 1981
La Chèvre, 1982
Danton, 1982
Le Grand Frère, 1982
The Return of Martin Guerre, 1982
Les Compères, 1983
The Moon in the Gutter, 1983
Wajda's Danton, 1983
Fort Saganne, 1984
Rive droite, rive gauche, 1984
Tartuffe, 1984
Police, 1985
Rue du depart, 1985
Une Femme ou deux, 1985
Les Fugitifs, 1986
Jean de Florette, 1986
Ménage, 1986
Under Satan's Sun, 1987
Camille Claudel, 1988
Deux, 1988
A Strange Place to Meet, 1988
Henry V, 1989
I Want to Go Back Home, 1989
Too Beautiful for You, 1989
Cyrano de Bergerac, 1990
Green Card, 1990
Uranus, 1990
Merci, la vie, 1991
Mon père ce heros, 1991
Tous les matins du monde, 1991
1492: The Conquest of Paradise, 1992
Francois Truffaut: Stolen Portraits, 1992
Germinal, 1993
Hélas pour moi, 1993
Colonel Chabert, 1994
My Father the Hero, 1994
A Pure Formality, 1994
Bogus, 1995

Later in his career, unconvincingly starving coal miner Depardieu (*far right*) displays ample—and we do mean ample—full-frontal nudity in *Germinal*, in which he's never too hungry to pass up making a pass at wife Miou-Miou (*second from right*).

translate the feeling of homosexuality rather than the act, and more interesting. Still, there was a big silence on the set when we were shooting the *plateau"*—the love scene between him and Michel Blanc. "The first kiss was *incroyable*, incredible."

Ménage came out in the U.S. on the heels of *Police*, in which he plays a tough yet tender cop who falls in love with a drug dealer's girlfriend. In *Police*, he slaps Sophie Marceau during an interrogation, and in *Ménage*, he slaps Miou-Miou for insulting her husband. "It was very difficult to hit the women," says Depardieu, looking ashamed, before coyly adding, "It is as difficult to hit as to kiss."

So, is Depardieu, like many of his characters, a mixture of tough and tender? He leans back, stubs out his Gitane. "Maybe . . ." he says, pondering. "*Oui, oui . . . absolument.*" Absolutely.

Lena Olin

Bowler, Stockings, and Killer Thighs

Mona Demarkov is bad. Not in the sense that Michael Jackson might sing it, but nasty, viciously bad. In *Romeo Is Bleeding* (1994), her hands are tied behind her back, she's been shot, she's in the backseat, but she needs to get out of the car and keep the loot. First, she wraps her killer thighs around the neck of the driver Gary Oldman, a dirty cop whose downfall has been those very thighs. Then, she manages to climb into the front seat, kick out the front windshield with her stiletto heels, grab the money case in her mouth, shimmy through broken glass, and hobble away. She kicks off her high heels as a parting gesture of freedom.

Romeo, directed by Peter Medak, features Lena Olin as a gleeful villainess in a bit of perfect casting. With her voice guttural enough to be a man's and that swaggering physicality, the Swedish stage actress has built up her sexual man-killing credits over several movies, notably *The Unbearable Lightness of Being* (1988) and *Enemies: A Love Story* (1991).

A serious actress, Olin, born in Stockholm in 1955, studied with and then worked for Sweden's Royal Dramatic Theater from age twenty. She collaborated with Ingmar Bergman so frequently that he wrote a part specifically for her in *After the Rehearsal* (1984).

Olin brings Euro-openness, Swedish blaséness, and a tinge of madness to her highly sexed roles; in *Lightness,* she habitually wears a bowler hat and black lingerie and nothing else as Daniel Day-Lewis's exhibitionistic mistress. "The nudity of the body or the nudity of the soul—it's part of the characters," she said after making that movie. "I'm not anxious to show my body, but it's not more big a deal than to show my eyes."

She was enticingly unbalanced in Paul Mazursky's *Enemies,* in which she played Holocaust survivor Masha, a reckless and passionate woman for whom sex is the key to existence. There are several topless scenes where she and occasional husband Ron Silver make love to remind themselves they're alive. "I am a very unsatisfied and restless personality," she admitted after *Enemies.* "I don't necessarily say I'm neurotic, and if I was, I don't hate it anymore because the most unneurotic thing I could think of is a stone."

She complained once that well-meaning people had given her silly advice: "That because I was so undressed people won't take me seriously."

In any case, Mona Demarkov is not meant to be taken seriously. She is so over the top that she becomes black comedy. "With or without?" she demands of a sex partner, meaning with the prosthesis for her missing arm strapped to her body or not; she has severed her own appendage to facilitate a lucrative con job. She buries a former lover alive, making her current lover pack down the dirt.

"Male screenwriters feel guilty about writing a bad woman," Olin says. "But I'm looking for egocentric female characters, women who do strange and awful things, because

(Opposite) Exhibitionist Lena Olin is her own obscure object of desire in *The Unbearable Lightness of Being.*

FILMOGRAPHY

Picasso's Aventyr, 1978
Karleken, 1980
Grasanklingar, 1982
After the Rehearsal, 1984
Pa liv och dod, 1986
Friends, 1987
The Unbearable Lightness of Being, 1988
Enemies: A Love Story, 1989
S/Y Gladjen, 1989
Havana, 1990
Fanny and Alexander, 1983
Mr. Jones, 1993
Romeo Is Bleeding, 1993

it's fun—and it's true."

Olin's movies tend to bomb when her character is not the one in the saddle. In *Havana* (1990), she plays second fiddle to Robert Redford; she's a revolutionary in 1958 Cuba, he's a high-stakes gambler looking for the last good time. If there had been as much chemistry between the two leads as there is sugarcane in Cuba, the $40 million Sidney Pollack movie might have lit a fire.

Then, there was *Mr. Jones* (1993), in which Olin played manic-depressive RICHARD GERE's frustrated therapist. It's a role she inherited when MICHELLE PFEIFFER backed out to crack the whip as Catwoman in *Batman Returns* (1992), a role she in turn inherited when ANNETTE BENING went off to have Warren Beatty's baby. *Mr. Jones* required Olin to fall prey to the charms of her emotionally teetering patient, but the sex is not erotic, knowing that Mr. Jones has more of a stake in leaning dangerously over high ledges.

From the evidence, it's safe to say that Olin is at her best when on top and unpredictable, teasing those panting, hapless men who want her to wrap those thighs around them—even if it is around their necks.

Method Nudity

STARS WHO REALLY GET INTO THE ACT

Sharon Stone scratches back in *Basic Instinct*, in which Douglas and costar forewent the "crotch patch" so that their sex scenes would look more realistic.

Michael Douglas

Forgoing the "Crotch Patch" for the Sake of Art

Michael Douglas never did reveal the exact training regimen he endured before making *Basic Instinct* (1992), a movie that for all intents and purposes costars his bare butt. Whatever he did, some people say it wasn't enough.

But that's a little unfair. It's not every day that a major Hollywood figure exposes his figure—and Douglas was just shy of fifty when he made the movie.

In *Basic Instinct*, Douglas plays a detective who can't keep his hands off murder suspect SHARON STONE. She has a way about her—or maybe it's just that she doesn't wear underwear in the interrogation room.

Premiere magazine reported that the costars declined to wear the usual "crotch patch" as the last line of defense between their bodies while filming those sex scenes; what noble efforts actors make to remain true to their art!

As a result, there are brief glimpses of full-frontal nudity during those

FILMOGRAPHY

Hail, Hero!, 1969
Adam at 6 AM, 1970
Summertree, 1971
Napoleon and Samantha, 1972
Coma, 1977
The China Syndrome (also producer), 1979
Running (also executive producer), 1979
It's My Turn, 1980
Tell Me a Riddle, 1980
The Star Chamber, 1983
Romancing the Stone (also producer), 1984
A Chorus Line, 1985
The Jewel of the Nile (also producer), 1985
Fatal Attraction, 1987
Wall Street, 1987
Black Rain, 1989
The War of the Roses, 1989
Shining Through, 1992
Basic Instinct, 1992
Falling Down, 1993
Disclosure, 1994
The American President, 1995

famous forty-five seconds of sex that were cut to achieve an R rating in the U.S. and which were promptly restored a few weeks later for the European release and the predictable "director's cut" video.

Those forty-five seconds of sex were unveiled at the opening night of the 1992 Cannes Film Festival. The next morning, although Douglas had been gung-ho about making the movie and doing his scenes without a body double, he was made visibly uncomfortable by all the interest his private parts had generated among the international press. He gave them the usual line about how filming a sex scene is hard, boring work. "Haven't any of you pretended to enjoy sex with someone?" he asked the room, which got very still. "Well, haven't you?" Er, no, Michael.

Douglas was born in New Brunswick, New Jersey, on September 25, 1944. Although he studied drama at the University of California and theater in New York, he established his early career behind the scenes as an assistant director on some of the films of his famous actor-father, Kirk. Later he was known primarily as a television actor, thanks to *The Streets of San Francisco.*

All that changed in 1975, when he produced *One Flew Over the Cuckoo's Nest,* a quality production that earned a best picture Oscar.

He combined the power of producing with the glamor of being a romantic lead in two enormously popular films with KATHLEEN TURNER, *Romancing the Stone* (1984) and *The Jewel of the Nile* (1985).

Power can be a drug, and he showed just how addictive that could be as a megalomaniacal stockbroker in *Wall Street,* winning an Oscar for his role.

Sex can be a drug, too, and Douglas nearly gets an overdose of it in *Disclosure* (1994), based on the outrageous Michael Crichton novel in which a female boss makes

unwanted sexual advances to her subordinate, who then forces a showdown in court. DEMI MOORE plays the power-mad sex abuser who wants to have her way with Douglas.

With the testosterone legacy from the career of his look-alike dad and the knowledge that he is in fact a Hollywood player, Douglas manages to convey on-screen a man of power and privilege, both of which are turn-ons. "He gives off sparks like a Van de Graaff generator," purred *Vanity Fair*. His soft almost jowly looks lend themselves to characters who have a fatal weakness; hence *Fatal Attraction* (1987), in which he lives (barely) to regret breaking his marriage vows.

Douglas may have gotten the butt-baring bug during that movie when he hoisted Glenn Close atop the kitchen sink and dropped his drawers. The movie became a touchstone for the lure, fear, and consequences of marital infidelity. It was perhaps a perfect role for the married Douglas, whose name is frequently in the gossip columns; the items imply that in real life, Douglas has foregone the crotch patch a little too often.

Are those Demi Moore's fingerprints, or are you just happy to see me? Michael Douglas tries to hide signs of sexual harassment from wife Caroline Goodall in *Disclosure*, a movie in which no one gets totally undressed, but Moore does a pretty good job of feigning fellatio.

Melanie Griffith

A Bod for Sin

With her baby-soft voice and voluptuous looks, Melanie Griffith has, as her character in *Working Girl* might put it, "a head for business and a bod for sin." Born August 9, 1957, in New York, she has parlayed her kittenish sex appeal into a career of gold-hearted vixens and undervalued strivers, most of whom have frequent opportunities to undress for the camera.

Undressing certainly makes sense in a movie like *Body Double* (1984), where Griffith plays a porn actress hired to do a sexy striptease for the benefit of the voyeur across the way. (That Griffith is the daughter of *Birds* actress Tippi Hedren probably made *Body Double* director and Hitchcock acolyte Brian De Palma's heart beat faster.) And undressing makes sense in *Something Wild* (1986), where Griffith plays the wild something who is teaching Jeff Daniels the ropes of bondage.

Teenage Melanie Griffith letting it all hang out in *Night Moves*.

FILMOGRAPHY

The Harrad Experiment, 1973
Night Moves, 1975
The Drowning Pool, 1975
Smile, 1975
Joyride, 1977
One on One, 1977
Roar, 1981
Body Double, 1984
Fear City, 1985
Something Wild, 1986
Cherry 2000, 1988
The Milagro Beanfield War, 1988
Stormy Monday, 1988
Working Girl, 1988
Bonfire of the Vanities, 1990
In the Spirit, 1990
Pacific Heights, 1990
Paradise, 1991
Shining Through, 1992
A Stranger Among Us, 1992
Born Yesterday, 1993
Milk Money, 1994
Nobody's Fool, 1994
The Gaslight Addition, 1995

Even in *Working Girl* (1988), a film about a woman who pulls herself up the corporate ladder by her garter straps, it adds to her character's winning cuteness when she does the vacuuming topless. And in *Milk Money* (1994), even though we don't technically see them, her breasts are the focal point of the movie, because Griffith plays a prostitute paid to reveal them to preteen boys who then take her home to Dad in suburbia.

Like having Lloyd's of London insure Betty Grable's legs, Griffith must have valued her breasts as a career asset. With that in mind, she went the extra mile for her role in *The Bonfire of the Vanities* (1990), having her breasts surgically enhanced just in time to play the mistress who contributes to Tom Hanks's downfall in society.

As Julie Salamon reported in *The Devil's Candy*, a nonfiction report on the making of one of the decade's great disasters, Griffith was missing in action for a few days between New York location shooting and L.A. interior shooting. She had yet to shoot her lingerie-clad love scenes with Hanks when she arrived on the set bigger and better than ever; the wardrobe department was the first to spread the word. When she pressed her chest into director De Palma's face, he pointedly refused to give her the approbation she craved.

It wasn't the only problem on that production having to do with Griffith's physical appearance. Cinematographer Vilmos Zsigmond was relentlessly cruel about the bags under the actress's eyes. He ridiculed how she had looked in *Working Girl*, when her face and body were puffy from a well publicized bout of drinking. He wished aloud that the part had gone to UMA THURMAN, who had tested for the role but whose libidinous reading made Hanks nervous. "When she showed up the whole crew went wild," said Zsigmond of Thurman. "I think this movie would have needed something like this."

It turned out the movie needed something a lot more than

that, because it bombed big-time and has joined the ranks of *Heaven's Gate* and *Ishtar* as one of the all-time cinema turkeys.

But as long as there are men who like their women sweet and girlish, there is an audience for Griffith. She may not have been the most believable wartime double agent in *Shining Through* (1992) or undercover agent among the Hasidic community in *A Stranger Among Us* (1992), but those were roles that didn't properly showcase the emotional fragility that makes men want to have her and protect her.

In *Nobody's Fool* (1994), Griffith plays the long-suffering wife of womanizer BRUCE WILLIS, but not quite so suffering that she doesn't take the opportunity to show just how well her surgery has held up. Griffith pulls up her sweater for her husband's employee, Paul Newman, who is completely unnerved by the sight, as men often are.

Hired stripper Griffith doesn't seem in need of those future implants as she feels up voyeur Craig Wasson in *Body Double.*

Photo courtesy of Photofest

Linda Hamilton

Pec's Bad Girl

Linda Hamilton may be small and wiry, but she's one tough cookie. Even in the romantic short-lived television series *Beauty and the Beast*, in which she falls for the beast (Ron Perlman) who saves her from a mugging and is then so grateful she has his baby in the second season, she's a tough New York district attorney, not a pushover for the first beastly face to come along.

When Hamilton plays tough, she really goes all out. To reprise her role of Sarah Connor in 1991 in the second *Terminator* movie, wherein she must help ARNOLD SCHWARZENEGGER protect her ten-year-old son from destructive futuristic machinery, Hamilton pumped up to give the maternal protective instinct a physical overhaul.

The size-two actress worked out for three months, six days a week, doing one hour of aerobics and two of weight lifting every day before making *T2*. "Arnold was so proud of me, he kept pulling up my shirt, showing me off,"

Linda Hamilton affects the killer-babe look for *Terminator 2*, in which her fetishistic sex appeal derives from muscle, sinew, and a lock-and-load attitude.

said Hamilton. Director James Cameron must have been proud of her, too; they lived together off-screen.

She was a sensitive waitress in the first *Terminator* movie in 1984, the one in which Arnold was a bad guy. Her topless love scenes with Michael Biehn were the only humanistic elements in the science fiction movie. While biding time in several lackluster movies before *T2*, she had a carnal love scene in *Black Moon Rising* (1986) with the usually unromantic Tommy Lee Jones.

In *T2*, she adopts the Tank Top Into Combat look made fashionable by SIGOURNEY WEAVER, and the only intimate parts of her anatomy you see are those fabulous muscles as she locks and loads with the best of them.

FILMOGRAPHY

TAG: The Assassination Game, 1982
The Terminator, 1984
The Stone Boy, 1984
Children of the Corn, 1984
King Kong Lives, 1985
Black Moon Rising, 1986
Mr. Destiny, 1990
Terminator 2: Judgment Day, 1991
Silent Fall, 1994
Separate Lives, 1995

Mariel Hemingway with the profile she pumped up surgically to get the role in *Star 80*, as doomed *Playboy* playmate Dorothy Stratten.

Mariel Hemingway

Augmenting Those Audition Techniques

Ernest Hemingway made a career of writing short, terse sentences. His granddaughter Mariel took the larger view. For her, bigger was better, so to convince director Bob Fosse that she was right to play doomed starlet Dorothy Stratten in *Star 80* (1983), she had her breasts enlarged.

The gorgeous Mariel had no need to look buxom in her first two movies. In *Lipstick* (1976), at age fifteen, she plays the innocent young sister of a rape victim (played by older sister Margaux Hemingway). And in *Manhattan* (1979), she plays the sweet high schooler who dates older man Woody Allen (obviously a harbinger of things to come for Allen).

In *Personal Best* (1982), the strapping, outdoorsy Hemingway had some full-frontal nude scenes as a track runner who begins a lesbian relationship with another woman on her team (Patrice Donnelly). Hemingway celebrated the movie and her own athletic prowess by posing nude for *Playboy* in an amber-lit full split.

FILMOGRAPHY

Lipstick, 1976
Manhattan, 1979
Personal Best, 1982
Star 80, 1983
Creator, 1985
The Mean Season, 1985
The Suicide Club, 1987
Superman IV: The Quest for Peace, 1987
Sunset, 1988
Fire, Ice and Dynamite, 1990
Delirious, 1991
Falling From Grace, 1992

Then, in 1983, she desperately wanted the role of slain *Playboy* playmate Stratten, murdered by the low-life husband who wouldn't let her go. Stratten had been living with director Peter Bogdanovich, and left him so bereft that he eventually married her younger sister, Louise Hoogstraten, who in turn had plastic surgery that she might approach Dorothy's physical perfection.

So, although plastic surgery would one day be a small part of the Dorothy Stratten story, Hemingway took the bull by the horns—to use an expression of which her grandfather would have approved—and augmented her talents up top.

The ploy worked, because Hemingway got the role and it remains probably her best film work. And because the role calls for the character to pose often for nude photos, the plastic surgeon's handiwork is frequently on display. "I hope people won't think this movie is about my breasts," said Hemingway at the time. "I did have the implants. But I didn't do it for the role. It was for me, truly."

Hemingway can still be daring. She shared a much-ballyhooed lesbian kiss with Roseanne on television in 1994. And yet she claims to be modest in her personal life. "I won't even wear a bikini on the beach," she has said. "You can't edit what you see on the beach."

Elle Macpherson

Egg Whites and Muscle

When ROBERT DE NIRO gains fifty pounds to play the aging Jake LaMotta in *Raging Bull* (1980), everyone's impressed. The poor man had to travel to Italy and force himself to have pasta and chocolate milkshakes for the sake of his art.

When supermodel Elle Macpherson does the same thing for her role as an earthy seductress in *Sirens* (1994), no one believes her.

And with good reason. There is a case to be made for an aging, beefy boxer past his prime to look genuinely out of shape, especially for a film that went on to be widely considered the best of the eighties. On the other hand, the role of an artist's model, who suggestively bites into forbidden fruit, sucks her fingers enticingly, and cavorts naked in the petal-strewn water, does not really require a vigorous campaign of overeating.

If Macpherson in her film debut gained the twenty pounds she said she did, they're all in her ample bust, which becomes the focal point of this erot-

Supermodel Elle Macpherson claims she gained twenty pounds for her role in *Sirens*, a movie that requires her to titillate Hugh Grant.

ic Australian comedy in which uptight Hugh Grant becomes quite unlaced at the sight of her.

The six-foot Australian model, born Eleanor Gow, isn't bad in her acting debut. (She previously had a walk-on in a boutique dressing room in 1990's *Alice*, allegedly because Woody Allen wanted to be near her and have a reason to have her partly undressed in a scene.) She has a pleasant voice, a direct gaze, a natural sense of humor, and is clearly comfortable with her long, lithe, but very womanly body. In fact, she is referred to in the modeling industry as "The Body," and began her career when she was spotted skiing during a vacation in Aspen, a more athletic variation on the discovered-at-Schwab's story.

"It's not a nude romp," Macpherson has said of *Sirens*. Yet, she announced that to appear more voluptuous, more like a real woman of the 1930s, she ate a low-fat, high-protein diet and worked out two hours a day for several weeks with a personal trainer. Normally, this is the regimen people use to *lose* weight, but perhaps supermodels are built differently.

"I ate things like egg whites, I gained a lot of muscle bulk," she said. "In the morning I'd take a shower and race past the mirror dripping wet so I wouldn't see myself in it."

Midway through filming, her Method sensibilities flagged, and she resumed her usual low-fat, high-carbohydrate diet so she would be ready to shoot the next *Sports Illustrated* cover, the job that pays her rent.

Macpherson back to her slim
self, post–*Sirens*, post–*Sports
Illustrated*, post–video workout.

*Photo courtesy of Albert
Ferreira/DMI*

FILMOGRAPHY

Alice, 1990
Sirens, 1994
If Lucy Fell, 1995

Penelope Ann Miller
"A Passion in Me"

I look for characters with complexity, with a story of their own. I am not interested in playing any sex object to a male character," announced Penelope Ann Miller.

How then to explain her role in *Carlito's Way* as Gail, a topless dancer in a tony strip joint who quickly falls back in love with the gangster ex-boyfriend who got out early on parole?

Miller was born January 13, 1964, in Los Angeles. Small and blond, with the wide-open face of an ingenue, she had never done anything as wild before playing Al Pacino's ex-girlfriend in *Carlito's Way*, a 1993 Brian De Palma movie that gives no motivation for her character to do all those hip-thrusting topless numbers except that it looks nice as window dressing for the movie. But like LAURA DERN in *Wild at Heart*, the role seemed to liberate the actress to move more freely in her skin, to get turned on when Pacino bangs down her door and forces himself on her.

To really get into the role, Miller committed the greatest sacrifice—she bedded her costar, the better to see how it feels to be his girlfriend. (Pretty soon, she also got to see how it felt to be his ex-girlfriend, because Pacino's longtime lover, Lyndall Hobbs, threw a fit when she found out.)

"Al is a very passionate person, and he brought out a certain womanliness, a sexuality, a passion in me," the former Tavern on the Green waitress and soap actress rhapsodized to *People* magazine.

This new passion, womanliness, and sexuality certainly found its way on-screen, because she and Pacino sizzle in a way that the attractive but white-bread Miller had never man-

Penelope Ann Miller puts some passion into her sex scenes with Al Pacino both on and off the set of *Carlito's Way.*

aged before. She had often played "the girlfriend"—the guarded girlfriend of ARNOLD SCHWARZENEGGER in *Kindergarten Cop* (1990), the neurotic gangster's daughter girlfriend of Matthew Broderick in *The Freshman* (1990), and the coldly careerist girlfriend of Danny DeVito (!) in *Other People's Money* (1991). "I'm the subplot," she complained about her roles to *Premiere* magazine. "I'm the one they come home to. I don't mind it, but I'm never really part of the action."

Raw sensuality only showed up in her work thanks to all that extracurricular studying she did with Pacino. It paid off again in *The Shadow* (1994); even though the movie bombed, Miller looked hot in clingy silk opposite ALEC BALDWIN.

Now that Pacino has released the beast in Miller, she wants to make sure everyone gets a good look.

Photo courtesy of Albert Ferreira/DMI

FILMOGRAPHY

Adventures in Babysitting, 1987
Big Top Pee-Wee, 1988
Biloxi Blues, 1988
Miles From Home, 1988
Dead-Bang, 1989
Awakenings, 1990
Downtown, 1990
The Freshman, 1990
Kindergarten Cop, 1990
Other People's Money, 1991
Year of the Comet, 1992
The Gun in Betty Lou's Handbag, 1992
Chaplin, 1992
Carlito's Way, 1993
The Shadow, 1994
Witch Hunt, 1995

Rear Projection

THE BUTT STOPS HERE

Kevin Costner

Directing Those Scenic Closeups of His Own Derrière

There are many impressive sights in *Dances With Wolves*, Kevin Costner's epic, multi-Oscar-winning 1990 directorial debut. Some people remember the extraordinary buffalo stampede. Some remember the glorious South Dakota locations. And some remember Kevin Costner's butt, splayed across the screen in Panavision.

Costner plays Lt. John Dunbar, a Civil War soldier who befriends the local Sioux near his lonely outpost and eventually joins their tribe. It is after he has scared away Kicking Bird that he stands there naked as a jaybird. His back is to the camera, which pulls back to take in every nuance and detail of the landscape—at the center of which is Costner's caboose.

What you have to remember about filmmaking is that things don't just happen up there on the screen at random. The director decides everything ahead of time, maps it out, discusses it with his cinematographer. A shot that lasts a few seconds on screen can take hours to set up and light. The director later decides which shots to include in the final edit and how long these shots should last.

Sometimes, actors fight with their directors about whether they should take their clothes off. The star complains that it's too embarrassing, personal, or unnecessary. The director wheedles that it's in the interest of art, makes a statement, shows the character's vulnerability. In the case of *Dances With Wolves*, star and director were in complete agreement. It was Costner himself who must have said something like, "Hey, let's have the camera linger lovingly on my butt!"

You can also see some rear projection of Costner in *American Flyers* (1985) and *Revenge* (1990). But in *Robin Hood: Prince of Thieves* (1991), Costner used his star power to bring in a body double to peel for those waterfall moments. He had already struggled through the scene where he drags himself ashore after his escape from prison, and didn't want the water torture again—filmed in merry but rugged olde England, where the temperature was too cold. Also, he was starting to chub out just a bit from the salutary effects of his *Dances with Wolves* fame.

In *No Way Out* (1987), notorious for the hot scene in which Costner and Sean Young negotiate the backseat of a limo, Costner also displays a brief flurry of pubic hair in a scene in which he wanders around the bedroom with his jeans undone.

Costner was born in Los Angeles on January 18, 1955, and studied marketing in college. His first film role was in the unreleasable *Sizzle Beach, U.S.A.*, which became releasable in 1986 on video only because Costner was famous by then. He is awkward in a fireside sex scene in which he seems to forget to take off his cowboy hat. In an early film, *Fandango* (1985), the camera is positioned between his legs looking up for a prolonged basket shot—blame it on the director, Kevin Reynolds, who later held the reins on *Robin Hood.*

Furry-chested Kevin Costner and Suzy Amis cavort on the beach in *Fandango*, a movie that takes time out to photograph Costner's basket by looking up from between his legs.

Somewhere in a vault there is unused footage from *The Bodyguard* (1992), in which Costner is not too guarded about his body. Whitney Houston plays the pop singer who pays for Costner's protective services, and the two fall in love—or, as Houston might say, "And I-ay-ay-ay-ay will always love you-oo-oo." Reportedly, the costars filmed an explicit sex scene, but the filmmakers chickened out at the last moment for fear that the interracial aspect would hurt the box office in certain regions of the country. What titillates one segment of the population can cause riots elsewhere, a common problem for film marketers.

FILMOGRAPHY

Sizzle Beach, U.S.A., 1974
Shadows Run Black, 1981
Chasing Dreams, 1982
Night Shift, 1982
Stacy's Knights, 1982
Frances, 1982
The Big Chill (scenes cut), 1983
The Gunrunner, 1983
Table for Five, 1983
Testament, 1983
American Flyers, 1985
Fandango, 1985
Silverado, 1985
No Way Out, 1987
The Untouchables, 1987
Bull Durham, 1988
Field of Dreams, 1989
Dances With Wolves (also copro-
ducer and director), 1990
Revenge, 1990
China Moon (coproducer), 1991
Robin Hood: Prince of Thieves,
1991
JFK, 1991
Truth or Dare (documentary), 1991
The Bodyguard, 1992
A Perfect World, 1993
The War, 1994
Wyatt Earp (also coproducer),
1994
Waterworld, 1995

The movie went on to become one of the biggest hits of 1992, thanks largely to female fans who bought into Costner's image as a stoic romantic figure fighting against his instinct to fall in love. If they ever make a "director's cut" with the love scene restored, there's a built-in audience awaiting it.

And speaking of double versions, for fans of Costner's manly chest, they can sample two versions of it—furry as a beast in a bathtub scene in 1994's ponderous epic *Wyatt Earp* and shaved clean as a whistle for his salad days earlier in the same movie.

Mel Gibson

A Bum Rap

Mel Gibson's short walk to the refrigerator in the first *Lethal Weapon* (1987) imprinted itself on the public consciousness, helping the movie cross over to the normally action-resistant female audience and thus become a big hit. Gibson gamely sacrificed his bare bottom to the greater needs of the box office, and he was well rewarded with two sequels.

But was it such a big sacrifice? Suddenly, Mel was dropping trou in nearly every movie. In *Bird on a Wire* (1990), Joan Severance sews up a buckshot wound in Gibson's tush, which Gibson claims had to be shaved for the scene because he is normally so hairy (a detail we could have done without knowing).

And there's the venerable Gibson rear end once again in *Forever Young* (1992) when he hauls himself out of a cryogenic chamber after having been frozen for a few decades.

Gibson has become synonymous with bare-butt shots, a running joke between him and his fans. Unlike many action heroes, however, he may have

Mel Gibson takes it on the chin and elsewhere in *Lethal Weapon*, a movie that opens with his bare butt and includes a homoerotic torture scene with **Gary Busey** applying the juice to the electrodes on Gibson's nipples.

FILMOGRAPHY

Summer City, 1977
Tim, 1979
Mad Max, 1979
Attack Force Z, 1981
Gallipoli, 1981
The Road Warrior, 1981
The Year of Living Dangerously,
1983
The Bounty, 1984
Mrs. Soffel, 1984
The River, 1984
Mad Max Beyond Thunderdome,
1985
Lethal Weapon, 1987
Tequila Sunrise, 1988
Lethal Weapon 2, 1989
Air America, 1990
Bird on a Wire, 1990
Hamlet, 1990
Forever Young, 1992
Lethal Weapon 3, 1992
The Man Without a Face (also
director), 1993
Maverick, 1994
Braveheart (also director), 1995

compromised his appeal to the gay audience because of homophobic attitudes that have been ascribed to him, like the mincing hairdresser he impersonates in *Bird on a Wire* (even though his first screen kiss, in 1976's *Summer City*, was with a guy).

But he probably picked up the sadomasochistic vote from his eroticized torture scene in *Lethal Weapon*, with a sneering Gary Busey at the controls. A bound Gibson is stripped to the waist, beaten, and hosed down before electrodes are attached to his nipples.

In person he is much smaller and more compact than he looks on screen, where his skill at playing brawny action figures in movies like *Mad Max* and the *Lethal Weapon* series has convinced audiences that he is larger than life. He is also not really as striking in person, unless that is because he was interviewed on a morning when he was chugging caffeine and Maalox in equal doses and his famous blue eyes were at half-mast.

The Australian—actually raised in Peekskill, New York, until he was twelve—may be eager to moon his audiences, but he actually dislikes doing sex scenes and tries to discourage them in his movies.

"It has to do with getting the right tone and not turning people off. You don't want to see too much of that. Once you get too gritty on certain levels, especially in action comedies, you lose that effervescent façade that you hope to create. You want to pull back a little from that."

Luckily, he didn't pull back from his hot tub scene with MICHELLE PFEIFFER in *Tequila Sunrise* (1988) or from SIGOURNEY WEAVER in *The Year of Living Dangerously* (1983).

But he and GOLDIE HAWN agreed to tone down the sexual element in the script for *Bird on a Wire*, figuring that sex should be confined "to your bed. Or somewhere else. On the kitchen table, I don't care. But sex on the screen makes me uncomfortable, and it's always being forced at you. Nudity itself doesn't bother me, that's all right. I mean, what's nudity?"

Woody Harrelson

Thereby Hangs a Hat

Woody Harrelson is adorable when he's dumb. And he hasn't gone out of his way, like ARNOLD SCHWARZENEGGER with his business acumen and SYLVESTER STALLONE with his *The Thinker* pose for *Vanity Fair*, to dispel the myth. Thus, he is the male equivalent of the bimbo.

The *Cheers* bartender's cheery indifference as to whether people perceive him as a dim bulb—even his *Cheers* character's name was Woody, a coincidence that further depersonalized him—allows fans the luxury of ignoring the Harrelson inner beauty and concentrating instead on the outer wrapping. His body is rangy, well built, and according to the Hollywood rumor mill, extremely well proportioned. He doesn't even seem to mind that last bit of gossip getting around, since he poked fun of it himself in *The Cowboy Way* (1994) when he is interrupted during a raucous sexual encounter and covers himself with the only thing at hand—a 10-gallon cowboy hat, which stays put without manual assistance, suspended as it is from nature's own hook.

Media-star serial killers
Woody Harrelson and Juliette
Lewis have as much appetite
for murder as for each other in
Natural Born Killers.

Harrelson has had love scenes with Rosie Perez, DEMI MOORE, and Juliette Lewis. With the exception of his serial murderer role in 1994's *Natural Born Killers*, he usually plays someone not far from his bartender alter ego—a loose, gregarious, playful chap, the kind who is willing to make funny faces with those elastic lips.

He was quite charming as a basketball scam artist in *White Men Can't Jump* (1992), where he plays dumb in order to get the stakes up before he cleans out his opponents. Unlike the usual glamorous, gauzily shot sex scene, girlfriend Perez orders him to take a shower before he gets into bed because he's so sweaty when he gets off the courts. "Man, you stink!" she yells as only people who are comfortable with each other can.

He's the one who rents out wife Demi Moore to Robert Redford for a million-dollar night of pleasure in *Indecent Proposal* (1993), although the only sex scenes in that movie involve Harrelson and Moore. "I'm close friends with Demi and with Demi's husband [BRUCE WILLIS]. You have to draw the line at how far to go, and I'm not good at drawing lines," said Harrelson of shooting the love scenes. "I like to be without boundaries. The scene was flesh and flesh coming together. I don't know if Demi was turned on, but me . . . But you have to think of what the repercussions will be. I don't want Bruce coming after me."

There's little danger of that, since Moore's most explicit scenes were shot with a stunt double.

Woody Harrelson's hands are where Rosie Perez, Demi Moore, and Juliette Lewis have been (in the movies), and where Glenn Close and numerous others have been (off-camera). And not for nothing, either—check out the fake Calvin Klein billboard in Times Square for the filming of *The Cowboy Way*—according to reports filtering from Hollywood, the "stuffed" look is actually quite realistic.

Photo courtesy of Albert Ferreira/DMI

FILMOGRAPHY

Wildcats, 1986
Doc Hollywood, 1991
Ted & Venus, 1991
White Men Can't Jump, 1992
Indecent Proposal, 1993
The Cowboy Way, 1994
Natural Born Killers, 1994
Money Train, 1995

Goldie Hawn

They're Playing Her Thong

As she giggles effervescently onto her fifties, Goldie Hawn looks better in many ways than she did when she established her public persona a lifetime ago as the dumb blonde of *Rowan & Martin's Laugh-In,* the 1968 television comedy show.

No one mistakes her today for dumb, even though she still plays zany comedy roles with gusto. By now, everyone realizes that she's had a parallel career as a producer, that she and longtime companion KURT RUSSELL have sternly held out against the institution of marriage because of their respective messy divorces, and that Hawn has a serious side that's not to be trifled with.

However, seriousness is not what people want from her. They want her to giggle and flash a little something, and Hawn is usually willing to oblige.

Even at an interview, Hawn—born Goldie Jean Hawn—is dressed in a white leotard whose scoop neck is so scooped that she needs to yank it up every now and then. In person and in several movies that feature gratuitous butt shots, Hawn is clearly proud of the dancer's body she has worked so hard to keep. She enjoys showing it off. "Working out makes me feel good," she says.

In *Overboard* (1986) opposite Russell, Hawn bends over in a thong swimsuit, offering a detailed view of the butterfly tattooed on her rump. Making that a trend, Hawn pulled the same trick on fellow drop-drawers MEL GIBSON in *Bird on a Wire* (1990), giving him an ample view as he follows her up a ladder in this otherwise fairly chaste action romance.

With that and some strip club dancing in *Crisscross* (1992), a movie Hawn put into production for herself, she established herself in the era following her 1980 *Private Benjamin* success as one of several stars who encourage idolization of their derrières. Next to Kurt Russell, the closest friend in Goldie's life is the StairMaster.

And yet she waxes philosophical on the subject of the representation of women's bodies on film and how that affects relationships with other actresses. "Women have been judged by their looks, by their age, by their youth most of the time," she declared after poking fun at herself by wearing a fatsuit in *Death Becomes Her* (1992). "We've always worked from a deficit, really, so that in itself creates a kind of competitive soil. It's the soil that creates a sort of distorted fruit. I personally never felt that way because I have good self-esteem, and I knew very clearly that no man would ever take care of me

Exhibitionistic former dancer Goldie Hawn finds reason for her blouse to gap even if it's only for Chevy Chase in *Foul Play.*

The plunging neckline is not just an aberration of the movies; Hawn keeps a low-cut profile wherever she goes.

Photo courtesy of Albert Ferreira/DMI

FILMOGRAPHY

The One and Only Genuine Original Family Band, 1968
Cactus Flower, 1969
There's a Girl in My Soup, 1970
$, 1971
Butterflies Are Free, 1972
The Sugarland Express, 1974
The Girl From Petrovka, 1974
Shampoo, 1975
The Duchess and the Dirtwater Fox, 1976
Foul Play, 1978
Lovers and Liars, 1979
Private Benjamin, 1980
Seems Like Old Times, 1980
Best Friends, 1982
Swing Shift, 1984
Protocol, 1984
Wildcats, 1986
Overboard, 1987
Bird on a Wire, 1990
My Blue Heaven (executive producer), 1990
Deceived, 1991
The Warner Bros. Story (documentary; cohost), 1991
Crisscross (also producer), 1991
Housesitter, 1992
Death Becomes Her, 1992

financially, even if I had to pick up trash in the street."

Luckily, she has never had to stoop any lower than it takes to doff an article of clothing. Hawn has worked steadily long past the age when there are meaty roles for women. And because of the Goldie Giggle, the only nudity she has done has been of the light romantic or playful kind. You won't see her in *9½ Weeks, Part II*.

Warren Beatty, who worked with Hawn in 1975 in *Shampoo*, reassured her that her looks—and therefore her career—would last. "Eat the right foods, take care of your body, because you're not going to age. *You* have the face that will stay young. It's the women with the cheekbones who won't."

Kurt Russell

It Takes Two to Tango & Cash

Perhaps to escape the embarrassment of all those bright-cheeked child-actor roles he played for years at Disney, Kurt Russell likes to project a man's man, he-man kind of image both on film and in his personal life. Those biceps bulging out of his famous muscle-T of *Escape From New York* were not for nothing.

The athletic, square-jawed Russell was born March 17, 1951, in Springfield, Massachusetts. He had hoped for a career in baseball but was sidelined by a shoulder injury. Although he is equally adept at comedy, Russell's image is perfectly captured by the Snake Pliskin character of *Escape From New York*—a tough-guy loner, a renegade pirate whose snake tattoo on his belly is a warning sign to all.

Even the fact that he and longtime companion GOLDIE HAWN have adjacent his 'n' hers ranch houses, and that he has a pilot's license and goes parachuting, reinforces the image. He actually enjoyed getting his eyebrows

259

The rugged, bicep-heavy look of Snake Pliskin in *Escape From New York* that made everyone forget Kurt Russell was once a child star in Disney movies. (Haggard Harry Dean Stanton can only wish.)

singed on the set of the hero-fireman flick *Backdraft* in 1991. "It's one of the few jobs I would choose if I weren't acting," says Russell, who did his own stunts on the movie. "And the reason is that you're doing something that really counts, and it's honestly exciting. It is truly a bona fide massively exciting experience to be in a room that is completely engulfed in flame, and you can die in it. It gets you going. You find out a lot about yourself, and I don't mean to confuse that with macho stuff."

Yet macho stuff is the very thing Russell projects. Which

FILMOGRAPHY

The Absent-Minded Professor, 1961
It Happened at the World's Fair, 1963
Guns of Diablo, 1964
Follow Me, Boys!, 1966
Guns in the Heather, 1968
Horse in the Gray Flannel Suit, 1968
The One and Only Genuine Original Family Band, 1968
The Computer Wore Tennis Shoes, 1970
The Barefoot Executive, 1971
Fools' Parade, 1971
Now You See Him, Now You Don't, 1972
Charley and the Angel, 1973
Superdad, 1974
The Strongest Man in the World, 1975
Used Cars, 1980
Escape From New York, 1981
The Fox and the Hound, 1981
The Thing, 1982
Silkwood, 1983
Swing Shift, 1984
The Mean Season, 1985
The Best of Times, 1986
Big Trouble in Little China, 1986
Overboard, 1987
Tequila Sunrise, 1988
Tango & Cash, 1989
Winter People, 1989
Backdraft, 1991
Captain Ron, 1992
Unlawful Entry, 1992
Tombstone, 1993
StarGate, 1994

is why when he and SYLVESTER STALLONE walk cheek-to-cheek into the prison shower in *Tango & Cash* (1989), they are very careful to have a scene in which they both demur over a dropped bar of soap. Russell doesn't mind posing for a little beefcake as long as it's understood that what he really means by being a man's man is that he's a woman's man.

(Above) Russell determinedly reprises the Snake Pliskin look right down to the eye patch for the comedy *Captain Ron*, notable for having Russell run around for two hours in his Speedo briefs.

Arnold Schwarzenegger

Pump Up the Volume

Austria-born Arnold Schwarzenegger has always taken a bodybuilder's pride in himself. Not so much pride, however, that he didn't try to stop *Spy* magazine from publishing a full-frontal nude photo of him in its March 1992 issue. The photo revealed the young Austrian in the kind of bend-and-flex pose that won him three Mr. Universe and seven Mr. Olympia contests, and also proves that not every muscle in the body has to be fully inflated to look presentable.

As the world's highest paid action movie star and a satellite by marriage of the Kennedy clan, Schwarzenegger hasn't been quite so keen to preen, at least not to the same degree. Although his body is truly his instrument, with those straining muscles and sculpted contours the true artistic focus of his work, he has only revealed his gluteus maximus in a couple of movies like *The Terminator* (1984) and the homoerotic sauna-to-snow fight scene that opens *Red Heat* (1988).

With the skill of a Meryl Streep doing different accents, Schwarzenegger, born July 30, 1947, has resculpted his body to adapt to the changes in his career. Although his cartoonlike bulk helped him get a foothold in Hollywood with such grunt epics as the *Conan* movies, his size was too off-putting for the more genteel public he also wished to court; he knew he would never make the switch to comedy, or at least to action comedy, without first scaling down a little.

Today, Schwarzenegger is totally reconfigured. Even his face appears remolded into classic planes and angles the better to catch the light. Most movie stars never admit to plastic surgery, but it doesn't take a rocket scientist to compare photos of Schwarzenegger, then and now, and notice a marked difference.

You could say he truly reconfigured his body to play a pregnant man in the comedy *Junior* (1994), for which he drew on wife Maria's pregnancies to imitate the heavy waddle, the back pains, and the waterworks hormonal surges. "Now I have my figure back," he joked after the movie, which actually contains some of his best acting.

With his famed expertise in finance and real estate, Schwarzenegger is just as savvy about how to use his body to maximize profits. "Challenges inspire me," he says. "I pick them in the first place. I look forward to tremendous obstacles, taking tremendous risks. Some of the

Arnold Schwarzenegger at his most pumped for *Conan the Barbarian;* compare with more recent photos to see how he has redefined his body to suit his career.

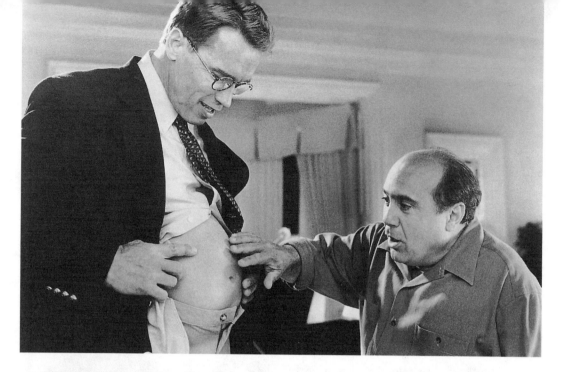

FILMOGRAPHY

Hercules in New York, 1969
Stay Hungry, 1975
Pumping Iron, 1976
The Villain, 1979
Conan the Barbarian, 1982
Conan the Destroyer, 1984
The Terminator, 1984
Commando, 1985
Red Sonja, 1985
Raw Deal, 1986
Predator, 1987
The Running Man, 1987
Red Heat, 1989
Twins, 1988
Kindergarten Cop, 1990
Total Recall, 1990
Terminator 2, Judgment Day, 1991
Feed (documentary), 1992
The Last Action Hero, 1993
True Lies, 1994
Junior, 1994

films come out not as successful as you hoped. There is no such thing as a smooth ride. It's one step back, two to the front."

He took one of those steps back with *Last Action Hero* (1993), which tried to humanize the Arnold image by taking him off the action screen and down into real life, where punches can hurt and people are mortal. Fans didn't go for it and the movie flopped resoundingly, weakening Columbia Pictures that year. It's a thin line that Schwarzenegger walks between advancing his career and turning off the fans who like him for being mythically invincible.

Arnold himself doesn't mind conveying that image. In *Pumping Iron*, the bodybuilding movie that in 1977 first introduced American audiences to the future box-office champ, he tells director George Butler how he trained himself "to be cold" in order to get ahead, and that pumping up his muscles "is as satisfying to me as coming. I'm coming day and night so I'm in heaven."

• •

(Above) It's not unusual to see Schwarzenegger's belly in the movies, only in the comedy *Junior*, he's in the third trimester.

• •

Memorable
Sex Scenes

SNAPSHOT ALBUM OF FAMOUS SEX SCENES
IN MOVIE HISTORY

(Above) Greta Garbo and John Gilbert practiced a lot off-screen to achieve that on-screen chemistry, obvious here in a still from *A Woman of Affairs* (1928).

(Top) Humphrey Bogart and Ingrid Bergman sacrifice their love of each other for the sake of the Cause in *Casablanca* (1942). Which is not to say the two do not commit adultery; no nudity, but the implication is clear as they close in for an embrace and the movie cuts to Bogart puffing an après-liaison cigarette by the window.

(Center) Richard Burton and Elizabeth Taylor carried their enthusiasm for their *Cleopatra* roles off-screen as well, starting an affair that proved far more interesting than the 1963 debacle they were shooting.

(Left) Dustin Hoffman loses his better judgment in the face of older woman Anne Bancroft's well-turned ankle in 1967's *The Graduate*.

(Left) Partly nude slave-boy Tony Curtis gives Laurence Olivier a frankly homosexual bath in *Spartacus* (1960), a scene that was only restored in 1991 (with Anthony Hopkins dubbing the voice of the late Olivier).

(Right) French bombshell Brigitte Bardot spent most of her formative years in the fifties and sixties in states of delightful undress. *Photo courtesy of Photofest*

(Left) Lusty Pole Marlon Brando gets the colored lights going with Kim Hunter in *A Streetcar Named Desire* (1951). The censors paled at the Tennessee Williams material and enforced two major changes—all mention was dropped of the homosexuality of Blanche's dead husband, and Stella leaves Stanley at the end despite frequent animal bellows of "Stella!" by Brando in his torn undershirt.

(Left) Marlon Brando and Maria Schneider find that quickie affairs go smoother with a little butter in *Last Tango in Paris* (1973), controversial even today because it showed a big star letting his fingers do the walking. *Photo courtesy of Photofest*

(Below) Humphrey Bogart and Lauren Bacall fall in love on and off the set of *To Have and Have Not* (1944), wrecking one of Bogart's marriages and making the movie known as one of the great love stories of all time.

(Left Center) Actress Maruschka Detmers actually performs fellatio on her costar on-camera in *Devil in the Flesh* (1986), giving new meaning to the phrase "chewing the scenery."

(Below Left) Isabelle Huppert, one of France's most frequently nude actresses, plots to kill Dad (Jean Carmet), in *Violette* (1978), based on a true crime story. No matter what the plot, French movies always have room for a topless scene or two. *Photo courtesy of Photofest*

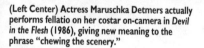

(Above) William Holden shows Kim Novak and her small-town neighbors a thing or two they haven't seen in 1955's *Picnic*, notable for Rosalind Russell ripping the shirt right off Holden's chest in a lust attack, and for his slow dance with Novak to the strains of "Moonglow." Holden at thirty-seven was actually so terrified of looking old and unsuited for the role that he demanded another $8,000 for the dance "stunt."

(Right) Mamie Van Doren plays a stripper aptly named Saxie Symbol in *Three Nuts and a Bolt* (1964), one of a succession of movies that costarred Van Doren's ample chest. *Photo courtesy of Photofest*

(Below) Sophia Loren and some of her best-known attributes, here with Alberto Sordi in the silly comedy *Two Nights With Cleopatra* (1953), in which Loren spends each night bedding her personal guard, then having him killed in the morning. *Photo courtesy of Photofest*

WE DO NOT want to see Robin Givens naked as she is here with Marco Hoffschneider in *Foreign Student*. They make a pretty picture as long as Givens doesn't try out her limited acting skills.

Wish List

STARS WHO SHOULD AND
SHOULD NOT UNDRESS

(Above) **WE DO** want to see what this gentleman in *The Road to Wellville* is seeing of Bridget Fonda, but for that you'll have to go back to *Single White Female*.

(Right) **WE DO** want to see both Kevin Dillon (*left*) and Ray Liotta naked. Liotta flashes his buns in *Unlawful Entry*, but here in *No Escape*, on a futuristic prison island with no women in sight, he and Dillon are awash in homoerotic subtext without any means of release.

(Above) **WE DO** want to see Stephen Baldwin (*right*) undressed. He obliges us in *Threesome*, where his dilemma is whether to sleep with the male roommate (Josh Charles), who craves his body or the female roommate (Lara Flynn Boyle) who equally craves his body. Judging by what we can see of the Baldwin corpus when he goes skinny-dipping, you can't blame either of them. As the brother of Alec and William, Stephen is almost genetically guaranteed to disrobe in the movies.

(Left) **WE DO NOT** want to see Meg Tilly naked, even though she has a beautiful, lissome body that remains totally on display in *The Girl in a Swing* (which should be retitled *The Naked Girl in a Swing*). But that teensy, mannered, little-girl voice brings to mind Alvin and the Chipmunks.

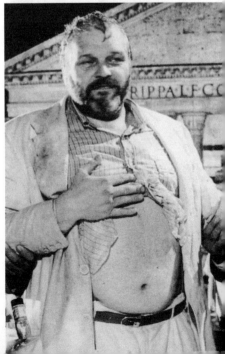

(Above) **WE DO** want to see more of *Dangerous Liaisons* costars Glenn Close (with major heaving bosom), John Malkovich (with deadly sneer), and Michelle Pfeiffer (with modestly heaving bosom). Michael Douglas pays a huge price for seeing Close's breasts in the thriller *Fatal Attraction*, while Pfeiffer has only barely revealed herself while getting dressed in *Into the Night*. But Malkovich, while balding and not conventionally handsome, put all doubts aside the moment his penis strode across the foreground in widescreen in *The Sheltering Sky*.

(Above Right) **WE DO** want to see Jeff Bridges naked, and not just that little bit of pubic hair sticking out of his waistband in this brooding publicity shot for *American Heart*. Whatever happened to the days when we could see his butt as a giant oak from a little DNA acorn he grew in *Starman*? We used to want to see his older brother, Beau, naked as well, but not since we saw him spray-paint his bald spot in *The Fabulous Baker Boys*.

(Below right) **WE DO NOT** want to see busy, portly character actor Brian Dennehy naked, especially not his overhanging belly in *The Belly of an Architect*. In that movie, we also catch sight of his buns as he gets down with Chloe Webb, another scene we can do without.

(Below) **WE DO NOT** want to see MTV dunderhead Pauly Shore's butt, as we do in *The Son in Law* when he moons his college classmates, nor do we want to see his chest, as we do here in a scene from *In the Army Now (second from left)*. Every generation is entitled to its sex symbols—unless it happens to choose someone like Shore, who calls food "grindage" and who looks like a Gumby.

(Above) **WE DO** want to see Jason Scott Lee naked, as often as possible. Here he is recreating the history of Easter Island in *Rapa Nui*, but it's well worth seeing the children's movie *The Jungle Book* just for that washboard stomach and pleasing proportions.

(Above) **WE DO** want to see more of Kirstie Alley after that teasing interlude in *Blind Date* (aka *Deadly Seduction*). The former *Cheers* star has the tawny mane and penetrating eyes most men would like to go to bed with and the irreverent sense of fun they'd like to wake up to.

(Below) **WE DO NOT** want to see Richard Harris naked, at least not now that he's pretty wrinkly, for his bare-assed swim in *Wrestling Ernest Hemingway*. It's a tush only costar Robert Duvall (right) could love.

(Below right) **WE DO** want to see Paul Newman undressed, any time, any place, any age—but maybe not in a toga like the one he wore in his film debut, *The Silver Chalice*.

(Above) **WE DO NOT** want to see any more of Armand Assante than is visible here in *Trial by Jury*. As charismatic as he is, that chest would be murder to groom each morning.

(Right) **WE DO NOT** want to see any more of Sean Penn than we have to, or than we saw in *Bad Boys*. Shown here in *Fast Times at Ridgemont High*, Penn has developed a reputation for being so pugnacious that it's not worth it to steal a peek if he's only going to punch your lights out for it.

(Below) **WE DO NOT** want to see Matthew Broderick naked, at least not as we see him in the disgust-o movie *The Road to Wellville*, in which Anthony Hopkins (right) makes fun of Broderick's penis size, and in which nurses of all stripes come by to give him enemas.

Acknowledgments

Writing a book like this brings out hidden talents in your friends. Who knew that Stephen Schaefer had so many anecdotes from the field? That Joe Leydon had such a deep appreciation of sex scenes? That Gerry Putzer had such an eye for detail?

In addition to these three, who gave freely and often of their time, much gratitude goes to the following people and institutions:

Scott and Barbara Siegel, who jokingly call themselves my "full-service agents," for going beyond the call of duty in shepherding this and other projects. More important, they are full-service friends, who sing to me on my birthday, bring me vitamin C when I'm ailing, show me the true path if not to enlightenment then at least to seasonal sales at Arche, and are not afraid to set me straight. (Well, they're a *little* afraid, but they plunge in anyway.) And they're not loathe to discuss one hundred more modest ways to say the word *penis*.

David McGough (and his dog Scooter) for kindly giving me permission to use photos by his talented DMI staff. There's nothing like candid shots of stars to illustrate how they perceive their personalities and bodies while off-screen.

Milton Goldstein, Frankie Leonardo, and Jose Diaz for flattering me into thinking I'm a Mac computer genius, or could become one in time.

RESEARCH: Chris Bowen for notes and quotes; James Pallot and Doris Toumarkine for turning me on to the Motion Picture Guide on CD-ROM; Doug Buffo for movie arcana and the safe haven of World of Video on Seventh Avenue

South; Diane Stefani of *Playboy* for knowing just how and when to connect people with the information they need; Ron Givens for his endless array of synonyms for the act of doing the horizontal mambo; film critic par excellence Dave Kehr for those same synonyms in French; Craig Hosoda and his *Bare Facts Video Guide,* the ultimate reference tool for voyeurs.

Plus, Cara White, Jeremy Walker, Steve Klain, Cynthia Swartz, Erica Steinberg, Mark Urman, Dorrit Ragosine, Frank Gaffney, Scott Levine, Mark Reina, Bruce Goldstein, Joanna Ney, Larry Steinfeld, Fritz Friedman, Louise Stanton, John Kelly, Nina Stern, Anne Stavola, Stu Zakim, Mary Lugo, Catherine Verret, Michele Maheux, Bruce Lynn, Pat Storey, Bingham Ray, and Ira Deutchman.

PHOTO RESEARCH: Howard and Ron Mandelbaum and the wonderful staff at Photofest; Russell Calabrese at Hi-Test Productions; Richard Neurohr and Rene Penco at Jerry Ohlinger's; Rita Zausner and Marilyn Lau. Special thanks for photos to all the kind folks at Paramount, Orion, Twentieth-Century Fox, Universal, Disney, Warner, Columbia, Miramax, Fine Line, October, Sony Classics, MCA Home Video, Warner Home Video, Columbia TriStar Home Video, and Buena Vista Home Video.

INDISPENSABLES: My patient, cheery editor at Citadel, Kevin McDonough; oh, commander mine, Steve Schragis of Carol Publishing; Mort Zuckerman and Martin Dunn for employing me at the *New York Daily News.*

FRIENDS: Amanda Kissin Low, Mark Hamilton, Marianne Goldstein, JoAnne Wasserman, Howard Feinstein, M. George Stevenson, Stacey Ross, Batton Lash, Sue Pivnick, Maria Umali, Ben Petrone, Ralph Donnelly, Fabiano Canosa, Tim Myers, Larry Friedman, Matthew Flamm, Jerry Tallmer, Ora

---

Geshensky, Jonathan Horne, Stephen Louis, Carole Lee, Salah Bachir, Larry Rosenthal, Arthur Schwartz, Lisa Tindall, Claudia Tindall, Mike Mooney, Lynn Samuels, Susan Shapiro, Larry Cohn, Tom Della Corte, Norman Bey, Terry Smolar, and the late, but still among us, Mason Wiley.

FAMILY: My parents Sam and Gloria Bernard, my sister Diane, and my parrot Sensei, who still dances the lambada while doing his famous "bombs over Dresden" noises whenever I try to nap.

About Last Night... (1986), *138*
Abril, Victoria, *202-5*
Adjani, Isabelle, *206-8*
Adlon, Percy, 158, 160
Alien series (1979, '86, '91), 39, *40*, 41
Allen, Woody, 60
Alley, Kirstie, *274*
Almodóvar, Pedro, 203-4
Altered States (1980), *94*
Altman, Robert, 109, 111
American Gigolo (1980), 89, *90*
American Heart, *273*
Amis, Suzy, *248*
Andrews, Julie, *44-47*
Angel Heart (1987), *67-68*
Ann-Margret, *166-68*
Assante, Armand, *275*
Atlantic City (1981), 25-26, *27*
Aykroyd, Dan, *154*
Bacall, Lauren, *268*
Backdraft (1991), 126
Backtrack (1990), *176*
Bacon, Kevin, *197*
Bad Boys, 275
Bad Girls (1994), *194-95*
Bad Lieutenant (1992), 101-4
Bad Timing: A Sensual Obsession
    (1980), 112-13
Baldwin, Alec, *169-71*
Baldwin, Stephen, *272*
Baldwin, William, *124-28*
Bancroft, Anne, *266*
Banderas, Antonio, 203-*5*, *209-12*
Bara, Theda, *xviii*
Barbarian, The (1933), *xiv*
Bardot, Brigitte, *267*
Barkin, Ellen, *74-77*
Barrymore, Drew, *48-50, 195*

Basic Instinct (1992), *145-46*, 147-
    48, *226*, 227-28
Basinger, Kim, *2-7*, 67, 170-71
Beals, Jennifer, *8-10*
Beatty, Warren, *14, 133-34*
Belly of an Architect, The, *273*
Ben-Hur (1926), *xi, xii*
Bening, Annette, *11-15*
Bergin, Patrick, 161, *163*
Bergman, Ingrid, *266*
Big Easy, The (1987), 75-76
Binoche, Juliette, 96, *213-16*
Bird on a Wire (1990), 250, 252
Bisset, Jacqueline, *16-18*
Black Widow (1986), 113-14
Blair, Linda, *51-53*
Blind Date, *274*
Blue Velvet (1986), 63-64, *65*
Body Double (1984), 231, *233*
Body Heat (1981), 36-*37*
Body of Evidence (1993), *79-80*, 134
Bodyguard, The (1992), 248-49
Bogart, Humphrey, *266, 268*
Bonet, Lisa, 67-68
Bonfire of the Vanities (1990), 232-
    33
Borden, Lizzie, 162-64
Born Innocent (1974), 51-52
Boyle, Lara Flynn, *272*
Branagh, Kenneth, 87
Brando, Marlon, *267, 268*
Bridges, Beau, *273*
Bridges, Jeff, *273*
Broadcast News (1987), 93
Broderick, Matthew, *275*
Brown, Blair, *94*
Bugsy (1991), *14*
Burton, Richard, *266*

Busey, Gary, *251*
Bye Bye Birdie (1963), 167, *168*
Cage, Nicholas, 22-23, *24*
Carlito's Way (1993), *242-44*
Carmet, Jean, *268*
Carnal Knowledge (1971), 168
Carter, Helena Bonham, 87
Casablanca (1942), *266*
Cates, Phoebe, *19-21*
Certain Sacrifice, A (1981), 133
Chained Heat (1983), 52, *53*
Charles, Josh, *272*
Chase, Chevy, *257*
China Moon (1994), 193, 194
Cleopatra (1917), *xviii*
Cleopatra (1963), *266*
Close, Glenn, 32, *35, 273*
Color of Night (1994), 119-20,
    121, 122
Conan the Barbarian (1982), *263*
Costner, Kevin, *246-49*
Cowboy Way, The (1994), 253,
    255
Crimes of Passion (1984), 38
Crossing the Line (1991), *180*
Cruise, Tom, *106-107, 172-74*
Crying Game, The (1992), *81-83*
Crystal, Billy, 84
Currier, Frank, *xii*
Curtis, Jamie Lee, *54-56*
Curtis, Tony, *267*
Dafoe, Willem, *78-80*, 134
Damage (1992), 96, 97-98, *213-
    15*, 216
Dances With Wolves (1990), 246-
    47
Dangerous Game (1993), *105*,
    134-35

Dangerous Liaisons (1988), 32-33, *35, 273*

Davidson, Jaye, *81-84*

Day, Doris, *xix*

Day-Lewis, Daniel, *192,* 194, *215,* 216

de Madeiros, Maria, *33*

De Niro, Robert, *34, 85-88*

Death and the Maiden (1994), 40

Death Becomes Her (1992), *198*

Deep, The (1977), *16*

Delaney, Dana, *150-54*

Demolition Man (1993), 142, *144*

Dennehy, Brian, *273*

Depardieu, Gerard, *85-86, 217-20*

Derek, Bo, *129-30*

Derek, John, 129-30

Dern, Laura, *22-24*

Detmers, Maruschka, *268*

Devil in the Flesh (1986), *268*

Dick Tracy (1990), 133, *134*

Die Hard series, *118,* 122

Dillon, Kevin, *272*

Dirty Dancing (1987), 199, 200

Disclosure (1994), 139, 228-*29*

Douglas, Michael, 139, *146, 226-29, 273*

Duvall, Robert, *274*

Ecstacy (1933), *x, xvi*

Edwards, Blake, 45-46

Enemies: A Love Story (1989), 222

Escape From New York (1981), 259, 260

Even Cowgirls Get the Blues (1994), 34

Exit to Eden (1994), 151, *152-54*

Exorcist, The (1973), 51, *52*

Fabulous Baker Boys, The, 273

Fandango (1985), 247, *248*

Far and Away (1992), *107,* 172-73, *174*

Farewell to the King (1989), *182*

Fast Times at Ridgemont High (1982), 19-*21, 275*

Fatal Attraction (1987), 229, *273*

Ferrara, Abel, 102-3, 134-35

Final Analysis (1992), *2*

Flashdance (1983), 8, *9*-10

Flatliners (1990), 126

Fly, The (1986), 57, 58, *59*

Fonda, Bridget, *272*

Foreign Student, 270

Foster, Jodie, *175-77,* 180

Foul Play (1978), *257*

Garbo, Greta, *266*

Garfunkel, Art, 112-13

Gaultier, Jean-Paul, *135*

Gere, Richard, *2, 89-92, 156,* 190, *191*

Germinal (1993), 217-19, *220*

Getaway, The (1994), 170-71

Ghost (1990), 138

Gibson, Mel, *250-52*

Gilbert, John, *266*

Girl in a Swing, The, 272

Givens, Robin, *270*

Glengarry Glen Ross (1992), 170

Goldblum, Jeff, *57-59*

Goodall, Caroline, *229*

Graduate, The (1967), *266*

Grant, Hugh, *240*

Grease, 72

Griffith, Melanie, 99-100, *230-33*

Grifters, The (1990), 11-*12*

Half Moon Street (1986), 40

Hamilton, Linda, *234-35*

Hanks, Tom, 211

Harlow, Jean, *xvi*

Harrad Experiment, The (1973), 99

Harrelson, Woody, *253-55*

Harris, Richard, *274*

Haunted Summer (1988), 115

Hawn, Goldie, *198, 256-58*

Hemingway, Mariel, *236-38*

Henry and June (1990), *33*

High Heels (1991), *202*

Hoffman, Dustin, *266*

Hoffschneider, Marco, *270*

Holden, William, *269*

Hopkins, Anthony, *275*

Hopper, Dennis, 64, *65, 176*

Housesitter (1992), 152, *153*

Hudson, Rock, *xix*

Hunt for Red October, The (1990), 169-170

Hunter, Holly, *102,* 104

Hunter, Kim, *267*

Huppert, Isabelle, *268*

Hurt, William, 36-*37, 93-95*

In the Army Now, 273

Indecent Proposal (1993), 139, 254

Interview With the Vampire (1994), *173-74,* 210, 211-12

Into the Night, 273

Irons, Jeremy, *96-98, 213-15,* 216

Jackson, Michael, *136*

Johnson, Don, *99-100*

Jungle Book, The, 274

Junior (1994), 263, *264*

Keaton, Diane, *155-57*

Keitel, Harvey, *101-5*

Kidman, Nicole, *106-8,* 173, *174*

La Reine Margot (1994), *206-8*

Lamarr, Hedy, *x, xvi*

Lancaster, Burt, *27*

lang, k.d., *158-60*

Last Exit to Brooklyn (1990), 131, *132*

Last of the Mohicans, The, 192, 194

Last Tango in Paris (1973), *268*

Lee, Jason Scott, *274*

Leigh, Jennifer Jason, *21, 131-32,* 170

Lethal Weapon (1987), 250, *251,* 252

Lewis, Juliette, *254*

Liotta, Ray, *272*

Lone, John, *97, 98*

Looking for Mr. Goodbar (1977), 90, 155, *156, 157*

Loren, Sophia, *269*

Love Crimes, (1992), 161, *162-64*

Lowe, Rob, *138*

Loy, Myrna, *xiv*

Lynch, David, 63

M. Butterfly (1993), *97, 98*

MacDowell, Andie, *195*

MacLachlan, Kyle, 63-64, *65*

Macpherson, Elle, *239-41*

Mad Dog & Glory (1993), *34*

Madonna, *79,* 80, *105, 133-36,* 209

Magic Garden of Stanley Sweetheart, The (1970), *100*

Maitresse, 219

Malice (1993), 108, 170

Malkovich, John, *273*

Man Trouble (1992), *74*

March, Jane, 119-20, *121*

Martin, Steve, *153*

Mary Shelley's Frankenstein (1994), *86-87*

Masterson, Mary Stuart, *195*

Max, Mon Amour (1986), 60, 62

Ménage (1986), 219-20

Mercurio, Paul, 152, 153

Miami Blues (1990), *170*

Midnight Cowboy (1969), *xx*

Miles, Sylvia, *xx*

Miller, Penelope Ann, *242-44*

Minnelli, Liza, 88

Miou-Miou, 217-18, *220*
Modine, Matthew, *110*
Moore, Demi, *137-40*, 254
Moore, Dudley, *130*
Moore, Julianne, *109-11*
Mr. Jones (1993), 224
My Own Private Idaho (1991), 188, 189
Naked in New York (1994), 115-16, 117
Name of the Rose, The (1986), 29-30, 31
Natural Born Killers (1994), 254
Neeson, Liam, 176, 177, *178-80*
Nell (1994), 176-77, 180
New York, New York (1977), 88
Newman, Paul, *274*
Nicholson, Jack, *186*
Night Moves (1975), *230*
Night Porter, The (1974), *61*, 62
9 1/2 Weeks (1986), *3-4*, 6, 67
1900 (1976), *85-86*, 219
No Escape, 272
Nobody's Fool (1994), 233
Nolte, Nick, *181-84*
Novak, Kim, *269*
Novarro, Ramon, *xi, xii, xiv*
O'Donnell, Rosie, 152-53, *154*
Ogier, Bulle, *219*
Olin, Lena, *221-24*
Olivier, Laurence, *267*
Otis, Carré, 66, *68-69*
Pacino, Al, 76, *242-44*
Party at Kitty and Stud's (1970), 141-42
Penn, Sean, *275*
Perez, Vincent, 206, *207-8*
Pfeiffer, Michelle, *185-87*, 273
Philadelphia (1993), 211
Piano, The (1993), 101, *102*, 104
Picnic (1955), *269*
Pitt, Brad, *173*, 174
Poison Ivy (1992), *49*, *50*
Preston, Robert, *44*
Pretty Baby (1978), *26*, 70-*71*
Pretty Woman (1990), 190, *191*
Prince of Tides, 183-84
Pulp Fiction (1994), 34-35, 122
Quaid, Dennis, 75-76
Rambo III (1988), *142*
Rampling, Charlotte, *60-62*
Rapa Nui, 274
Rea, Stephen, *81-83*

Redford, Robert, 139, 254
Reeves, Keanu, *188-89*
Reinhold, Judge, 19, 21
River Wild, The (1994), *197*
Road To Wellville, 272, 275
Roadhouse (1989), 199, *200*
Roberts, Julia, *190-91*
Roeg, Nicolas, 112, 113
Romeo Is Bleeding (1994), 221, 222
Rossellini, Isabella, 63-65
Rourke, Mickey, 3-4, 6, *66-69*
Russell, Kurt, 256, *259-61*
Russell, Theresa, *112-14*
S.O.B. (1981), *44*, 45-46
salmonberries (1991), *158-60*
Sarandon, Susan, *25-28*, 71
Schneider, Maria, *268*
Schwarzenegger, Arnold, 55, 141, *262-64*
Sea of Love (1989), *76*
Send Me No Flowers (1964), *xix*
Shadow, The, 171
She Done Him Wrong (1933), *xvii*
Sheltering Sky, The, *273*
Shields, Brooke, *70-72*
Shore, Pauly, *273*
Short Cuts (1993), *109-10*, 111, 132, 195
Siesta (1987), 75, 76
Silkwood (1983), 196
Silver Chalice, The, *274*
Single White Female (1992), 131, *272*
Sirens (1994), *239-40*
Skerrit, Tom, *49*
Slater, Christian, *29-31*
Sleep With Me (1994), *117*
Sliver (1993), *127-28*, 146, 147
Smooth Talk (1985), *23-24*
Son in Law, The, *273*
Sordi, Alberto, *269*
Spartacus (1960), *267*
Specialist, The (1994), *143*, 144, 146, 148
Speed (1994), *189*
Stallone, Sylvester, *141-44*, 148, 261
Stanton, Harry Dean, *260*
Star 80 (1983), *236*, 237, 238
StarGate (1994), *83*, 84
Starman, *273*
Steel, Dawn, 92
Stoltz, Eric, *115-17*
Stone, Sharon, 127-28, *145-48*, *226*, 227-28

Stowe, Madeleine, *193-95*
Streep, Meryl, *196-98*
Streetcar Named Desire, A (1951), *267*
Streisand, Barbra, 183-84
Swayze, Patrick, 138, *199-200*
Tango & Cash (1989), 142, 261
Tarzan, *xv*
Taylor, Elizabeth, *266*
10 (1979), *130*
Terminator series (1984, 91), *234-35*
They Can Kill You But They Can't Eat You, 92
Three Nuts and a Bolt (1964), *269*
Threesome, 272
Thurman, Uma, *32-35*
Tie Me Up! Tie Me Down! (1990), 203-5, 209, *210*
Tilly, Meg, *117*, 272
To Have and Have Not (1944), *268*
Tomei, Marisa, 30
Trial by Jury, 275
True Lies (1994), 54-55, 56
Truth or Dare (1991), 133-34, 209
Turner, Kathleen, *36-38*
Two Nights With Cleopatra (1953), *269*
Unbearable Lightness of Being (1988), *215*, 216, *222*
Unlawful Entry (1992), 194, *272*
Untamed Heart (1993), *30*
Valmont (1989), 11, 12, *13*
Van Doren, Mamie, *269*
Vanity Fair, 137-38, 158
Vargas, Valerina, 30
Victor/Victoria (1982), 46
Violette (1978), *268*
Voight, Jon, *xx*
Wasson, Craig, 233
Weaver, Sigourney, *39-42*
Webb, Chloe, *273*
Weissmuller, Johnny, *xv*
West, Mae, *xvii*
Whore (1991), *113*, 114
Wild at Heart (1990), 22-23, *24*
Wild Orchid (1990), *68*
Willis, Bruce, *118-22*
Wolf, *186*
Woman of Affairs, A (1928), *266*
Woods, James, 162
Wrestling Ernest Hemingway, *274*
Wyatt, Jim, *177*
Yanks (1979), *91*
Young, Sean, *161-64*

About the
Author

Jami Bernard is a film critic for the *New York Daily News* and author of *First Films: Illustrious, Obscure and Embarrassing Movie Debuts* (Citadel Press). Her biography of director Quentin Tarantino will be available fall 1995 from HarperCollins, and her film essays will be included in the National Society of Film Critics' 1995 anthology from Mercury House. She is a member of the NSFC and a member and past chair of the New York Film Critics Circle. Her work has appeared in numerous publications, including *Mirabella*, *Self*, and the *Washington Post*, and she has been a guest critic for CNN and the BBC. Previously she was the chief film critic for the *New York Post*.